Online
Market
Research

Online Market Research

Cost-Effective Searching of the Internet and Online Databases

John F. Lescher

Addison-Wesley Publishing Company

Reading, Massachusetts   Menlo Park, California   New York
Don Mills, Ontario   Wokingham, England   Amsterdam   Bonn
Sydney   Singapore   Tokyo   Madrid   San Juan   Paris   Seoul
Milan   Mexico City   Taipei

Many of the designations used by manufacturers and sellers to distinguish their products are claimed as trademarks. Where those designations appear in this book, and Addison-Wesley was aware of a trademark claim, the designations have been printed in initial capital letters or all capital letters.

The author and publisher have taken care in preparation of this book, but make no expressed or implied warranty of any kind and assume no responsibility for errors or omissions. No liability is assumed for incidental or consequential damages in connection with or arising out of the use of the information or programs contained herein.

Library of Congress Cataloging-in-Publication Data

Lescher, John F.
    Online market research : cost-effective searching of the Internet and online databases / John F. Lescher.
        p. cm.
    Includes index.
    ISBN 0-201-48929-5
    1. Marketing research—Computer network resources.   2. Online databases.   3. Internet (Computer network)   I. Title.
    HF5415.2.L45   1995
    658.8'3'028546—dc20   95-4739
                                                                              CIP

Sponsoring Editor: Kim Fryer
Project Manager: John Fuller
Production Coordinator: Ellen Savett
Cover Design: Suzanne Heiser
Set in 11 point Trump Mediaeval by Michael Wile

1 2 3 4 5 6 7 8 9-MA-9998979695
First printing, September 1995

Addison-Wesley books are available for bulk purchases by corporations, institutions, and other organizations. For more information please contact the Corporate, Government, and Special Sales Department at (800) 238-9682.

Contents

v

Foreword

by Alice Sizer Warner

Market research pays off. A giant part of market research is finding out what already has been done, has been written, about wherever it is that you sell and about those to whom you sell. Those who base their selling on thorough market research are profitable, are successful. What you will read in this book is how to take advantage of online tools to help you, yourself, to do market research.

This book is appropriate for the market researcher who wants to learn more about how to use online resources, and for the online searcher who wants to learn more about market research.

This book is also for the informed person with general interest in research who wants to learn more about what is going on, and for the student of information science trying to make sense of our vast array of available tools.

This is a practical, how-to business book. This is not a book about "cruising," "playing games," or "superhighways"; not about "wild wild worlds," "worms," or "yahoos."

In this book we are told the difference between primary and secondary marketing research, and about the effectiveness of online databases for secondary marketing research. Professional online services are described, as are use of the Internet and the World Wide Web for business research. The characteristics of consumer services are outlined, and we are told how to use those services as well. There are chapters on a researcher's responsibilities for data quality and on legally procuring the full text of a document whose existence is discovered via an online search.

For those of us who learn best through specific examples, we will find them. Throughout, the author uses his own experience in carrying out the online searching maneuvers specifically necessary to writing this book. He shows us how he did his own marketing research. He helps us to learn by his own example.

This book admits that our online tools are in their infancy. Whatever knowledge we have today will need to grow, to expand, to change. Nothing is static. The tool that is the Internet is a special challenge. The sheer size of the Internet and its exponential rate of change are enormous problems.

I have had the privilege of reading this book in manuscript at various stages of development. This book confirms my opinion of the author, with whom I had until now been acquainted as a lecturer and teacher. John Lescher knows where he has been, he knows where he is going, he recognizes when he gets to where he is going, and he is delighted to take us with him. He calls shots as he sees them, and explains what he sees in language even I can understand.

Acknowledgments

There are many people whose ideas and thoughts have helped me and influenced my writing. Amelia Kassel read an early outline, performed technical editing, and provided valuable inputs. My editor, Kim Fryer, has been a pleasure to work with.

Two people, however, stand out. One is Alice Sizer Warner, a wonderful person whose advice and support were invaluable. The other is my partner in life and best friend, Chris Towle. She continuously provided support and put up with paper everywhere during the writing of this book. She also read and commented on every page, greatly improving the quality of the book.

Thanks to them all.

Introduction

Save Time and Money: Perform Secondary Market Research Using Online Sources

The book you are reading is two things:

- A guide for businesses to online sources of information for cost-effective marketing research. Using this book, businesspeople can do marketing research cheaper and faster.
- A guide for online searchers and librarians to secondary marketing research. The book enables the trained searcher to better support the information needs of business.

Business managers, market researchers, librarians, competitive intelligence practitioners, students, and information professionals will learn to perform more cost-effective market research and to keep up with the rapidly changing environment.

This book provides methods and examples for the market researcher to efficiently access the valuable and relatively inexpensive data available online. It discusses the necessity of cost-effective marketing research. It defines the types and uses of data for secondary marketing research. It tells you

- what data is available,
- where to find that data online, and
- the types and characteristics of the various online data sources.

The book reviews the use of the following in secondary marketing research:

- Professional database vendors such as DIALOG, Dow Jones, and LEXIS-NEXIS (Professional databases are the best sources for time-sensitive and complete research.)
- The Internet
- Consumer services like CompuServe

It describes tools and gives examples of research performed using these sources. The book discusses the importance of training and planning when preparing to use online sources. A proven methodology for the difficult task of keeping up with locations of the newest and best data is provided, instead of a rapidly out-of-date "Yellow Pages." The book offers answers to important questions such as these:

- What are the researcher's responsibilities and tools for ensuring the quality of data provided?
- How are documents obtained—now and in the future?
- What are the legal, ethical, and copyright issues?
- How will the use of online information change in the future?

How to Use This Book

The book can be read straight through, or individual chapters can be used for reference. *Online Market Research* starts with an introduction to secondary marketing research in Chapters 1 and 2. Chapters 3 and 4 discuss where marketing research information may be found. The basic search skills needed for online research are presented in Chapter 5. Chapters 6 through 14 present the various online sources, their characteristics, and examples of their use. Chapter 15 discusses how to keep up with all the changes and growth of online sources. The important data quality, document-delivery, and legal issues are covered in Chapters 16, 17, and 18. The final chapter discusses the future trends and directions that will affect the use of online sources for marketing research.

> Added information, tips, quotes, definitions, and references are offered in boxes.

In the body of the book, boxes (like the one on this page) offer added information, tips, quotes, definitions, and references. At the end of most chapters, the section "For Further Reading" provides information on references cited in the text and lists additional sources I like and use.

The author may be contacted by E-mail at jfl@vivamus.com. Readers can find updated Web site information at http://www.vivamus.com.

1 | *Obtaining Marketing Data from Online Sources*

This chapter is an introduction to using online sources for marketing research. It provides a definition of marketing research and discusses its importance to businesses of all kinds. It presents an overview of using online sources to obtain data for secondary marketing research.

Why Do Marketing Research?

Successful businesses are customer-driven, market-oriented, and cost-efficient. Marketing maximizes company profits and protects a company's position against new competition. Marketing improves performance even if a company is lucky enough to have built the world's best mousetrap. Marketing research yields the knowledge a company needs for the best marketing.

In today's rapidly changing business and information environments, market knowledge is increasingly valuable. Companies are quickly introducing more new products and services to broader markets. Technology is spreading swiftly. Acquisitions, ownership changes, and mergers bring new and different competitors to markets. Companies are expanding into international markets. Rapid changes and increasing information needs require more comprehensive and timely marketing research.

The reengineering of companies increases their effectiveness and reduces the costs of basic business functions. Companies frequently achieve such innovation by applying new information technologies. Because marketing is one of the most information-intensive functions in business, it is a prime candidate for reengineering. The effective use of online research is an important element in that process.

Companies achieve cost efficiency in marketing research by using quality secondary marketing research (information from publicly available sources). While companies spend most of their money on primary research (information obtained directly from the customer), secondary research avoids repetition of work already accomplished and provides direction to the primary research plan. A fast and cost-effective method of performing secondary market research is using various online sources.

Marketing research is important to both new and ongoing businesses—and for both mature and new products. Most businesses, whether established or entrepreneurial, achieve success with a customer- and market-oriented approach. Companies should perform marketing research when starting a new business, when introducing a new product or service, or when maintaining a current business—in other words, all the time!

It is vital to have cost-effective marketing research. According to the *1994 American Marketing Association Survey of Marketing Research*, spending has increased significantly from 1988 to 1993. The average marketing research budget increased by 7percent. The growing importance of marketing research is not limited to the United States. In Canada, spending on research grew by 5 percent from 1992 to 1993. In the United Kingdom, spending grew even faster, at 10 percent. When the 1994 annual sales of firms doing market research and analysis in the United States are currently greater than $5 billion, attention to efficiency provides significant profit gains.

What Is Marketing Research?

Marketing research is the process that companies use to answer key questions like these:

- What is the economic environment?
- What laws and regulations apply to my product?
- Who are the competitors?
- What are their products and strategies?
- Where are the customers?
- Who will buy and why?
- What is my competitive advantage?
- What is the sales forecast?
- Is my advertising working?
- Do people like or need my product?

Marketing research is the gathering and evaluation of data regarding consumers' preferences for products and services. It is the organized use of sample surveys, polls, and other techniques to study market characteristics and improve the efficiency of sales and distribution. It was developed in the United States in the early twentieth century and spread rapidly after World War II to Europe and Japan. An overview of the marketing research process appears in Figure 1-1.

Marketing research starts with careful planning. Before research begins, both goals and resources are defined. That saves money and time. Then the researcher uses the two

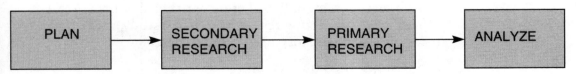

Figure 1-1 The marketing research process starts with planning and ends with analyzing and reporting the data

data sources described next to obtain the information defined in the plan.

- Secondary research is the collection and use of applicable existing data—from both internal and external sources. Secondary research, when performed first, provides information for planning and guiding the primary research task.

- Primary research is the direct collection of data from potential or existing customers through such means as surveys, interviews, focus groups, or point-of-sale tracking. Primary research is focused directly on the current research task and is often quite expensive.

> "[S]econdary research . . . saves time, saves money, and directs you to the next step. It often keeps you from reinventing the wheel. It can even tell you that the wheel you need hasn't been invented yet."
>
> —From *"Second Hand Prose,"* by Susan Detwiler, in *Marketing Tools*, January/February 1995, p. 12

When most marketing researchers start planning, their thoughts turn to primary methodologies. They often leave out secondary research, which can frequently provide results at lower costs. Secondary research is very cost-effective because it frees you from repeating previously performed research—you learn from experience. It also provides the information needed to plan and carry out the most effective primary research. According to Czinkota and Ronkainen, writing in *International Trade Forum*, insufficient knowledge is the single biggest reason for failure in the international marketplace, and the key to solving this problem is secondary research. Blair Peters, writing about the AMA-ARF 1993 marketing research industry study, identified key issues for satisfactory marketing research:

- Provide high-quality data
- Be on time with up-to-date data

- Provide an independent viewpoint
- Provide information that makes an impact on decisions or the bottom line
- Communicate
- Be team players

The final step in the process is the analysis and presentation of the information found. This book focuses on secondary marketing research performed using online information sources. Many sources provide additional information on the other phases of marketing research.

Where Can You Find Secondary Marketing Research Data? An Overview

Information on the latest trends, competitive data, demographics, product information, and other important topics is readily available. You can find your competitor's product introductions and marketing strategies and client and agency activities when you need to analyze new strategies, evaluate new product promotions, or plan a new ad campaign. Results from existing consumer research are accessible to you. Good information sources include

- Demographic data
- Industry analysts' reports
- Newsletters
- Marketing research studies
- Newspapers
- Press releases
- Product release information
- Public opinion polls
- Trade magazines

These are available from the vendors and locations listed below. This book focuses on secondary research from online databases, where information from all of the sources just listed can be found.

- Online databases
- Information specialists
- Libraries
- Market research firms
- Interviews, polls, focus groups, and experts
- Trade associations
- CD-ROMs

What Data Is Available? —An Introduction

The Economic Environment

Say you want to describe the economic environment with data such as nominal financial numbers and ratios for your industry, industry size, the companies in the industry, and important government regulations. Marketing research can identify the conditions and trends for economics, legal issues, rules and regulations, the state of the art of applicable technologies, social issues, and environmental issues.

Initially, you should establish an awareness of the shape of your industry and your market. Is the market growing or shrinking? How are demographics affecting its size? Are new competitors emerging or are old ones disappearing? Can market share be increased by selling to new consumers, or must your market share be achieved by wresting customers from your competition? Are significant new products being rapidly developed, or is the focus on minor improvements to an industry standard? Industry newsletters are valuable information resources for these topics.

Another key area is government regulations. Are they likely to be increased or relaxed? Research, using a variety of sources, will prevent unpleasant surprises. Many newsletters that follow regulatory trends are available through online databases. (For example, NewsNet provides access to newletters such as *Congressional Activities* and *Congressional Research Report*.) You can find publications such as those from the Bureau of National Affairs which cover legislative activities as well as regulatory agency pronouncements. The LEXIS-NEXIS online service includes databases that allow tracking of issues and bills through congressional committee hearings. Of course, the *Federal Register* is online (on DIALOG and LEXIS-NEXIS) and is easily searched for notices of proposed regulations, meetings, and final rulings.

Your Market

Successful companies understand and analyze their market. Data should include information on distribution channels, pricing, promotion methods, and market risk. You must learn about the need for a product, understand or define how your solution fills the need, project how the market will grow, and estimate the overall market size. Identify potential customers and their key decision makers.

If you produce a consumer product or service, census and demographic data are valuable information sources. The database Cendata (available on DIALOG), produced by the Census Bureau, can alert you to recently released reports of interest. In addition, numerous organizations, such as Claritas, provide detailed analyses and project demographic changes. That information is published in commercial reports and reported in newspapers, press releases, trade journals, and periodicals that focus on population dynamics, such as *American Demographics*.

If you sell principally to businesses, you must be aware of not only your market but also your customers' market. For instance, if many of your clients are in public relations and advertising, you would want to consider how the overall economy and the latest postal rate increase are affecting their business—and, in turn, yours. An analysis that focuses on the key trade journals for your customers' industries can provide you with facts about events and experts' interpretations of their impact.

The Competition

Information about competitors helps determine market risk and offers insight into distribution channels, pricing, and promotion methods. There are always competitors even if you have a unique solution to a problem and are first to market. You must know how the need is being filled now (What solutions are you replacing?). You must understand what your lead time is with respect to copycats and what barriers to entry exist (for both you and your competition). You must anticipate responses. By the time a press release comes out on your competitor's revolutionary product, it is probably too late for you to respond effectively. Yes, you may change your plan, but you really have lost a competitive edge. There are ways to anticipate at least the direction of product developments. For example, patent searches in the United States and in Europe will reveal potential new products. (In Europe the patent process is much speedier. Patent applications are published in eighteen months. Your competitor's application may be accessible to you before the U.S. patent is granted.) Research publications by employees of your competitors, available in scientific databases, will reflect their areas of interest and activity.

If direct competitive products exist, you must compare price, quality, and features. Locate articles on competitors to keep an eye on what they are planning. Find out whom your competitors are targeting for sales and on what areas they are focusing. Find out what their clients like or dislike about them. One easy way to track new competitors is through industry directories. For some industries in which most companies are small and private, directories and the Yellow Pages are virtually the only sources for discovering competitors. Association directories, buyers' guides from trade magazines, and product announcement press releases will alert you to the existence of new companies in your industry. The next step is to determine who they are: a start-up, an existing company with a new division or product line, or the subsidiary of a foreign company. Trade journals, SEC filings and brokerage reports (for public companies), regional business newspapers, and daily newspapers carry information on a company's financing, product line, and marketing strategy.

When you have identified your competition, you can obtain the needed information from many databases. The Dow Jones News/Retrieval Service can provide information on stock prices, new issues, executive changes, and articles in publications such as the *Wall Street Journal.* CompuServe allows easy and inexpensive capture of mentions of the companies in the AP and UPI wire services. NewsNet retrieves articles from industry newsletters. Many databases available on the Knight-Ridder DIALOG Information Services system carry data from trade magazines, national newspapers, and press releases. Which source is most effective depends on

- The size of your competitors
- Whether they are public or private (Private companies are more difficult to research and require more effort and skill.)
- Your specific industry
- The type of information about your competitors that will be the most useful

Summary

In this chapter, I have discussed the value of cost-effective marketing research and the important role secondary research plays. I have reviewed the various sources available for online marketing research and have looked at examples of typical research.

For Further Reading

> This section appears at the end of each chapter and provides cited references and other references I use and like. You will find them useful for additional information.

1. *Look Before You Leap: Market Research Made Easy*, by Don Doman, Dell Dennison, and Margaret Doman (Self-Counsel Press, 1993). A good introduction to marketing research, both primary and secondary. Easy to read.

2. *Do-It-Yourself Marketing Research*, by George Breen and A. B. Blankenship (McGraw-Hill, 1989). Another good introduction to marketing research, with lots of examples.

3. "Second Hand Prose," by Susan Detwiler, in *Marketing Tools*, January/February 1995, p. 12. Susan Detwiler and Associates is an independent search firm serving the health and medical industry. They publish *The Detwiler Directory of Medical Market Sources*, a 512-page road map to the health-care information industry. For more information, contact them at P.O. Box 15308, Fort Wayne, IN 46885-5308; 219-749-6717.

4. "Market Research for Your Export Operations: Part I—Using Secondary Sources of Research," by Michael R. Czinkota and Ilkka A. Ronkainen, in *International Trade Forum*, no. 3, 1994, pp. 22–33 (ISSN: 0020-8957). A very good article about the value of secondary sources in marketing research.

5. "AMA-ARF Study Reveals Industry Trends," by Blair Peters, in *Marketing News*, June 6, 1994, p. 14 (ISSN: 0025-3790). Good review of an industry standard study.

6. *Survey of Marketing Research*, edited by Thomas C. Kinnear and Ann R. Root (American Marketing Association, 250 South Wacker Drive, Chicago, IL 60606, 1995). The standard survey of marketing research, with information on how companies organize for marketing research, budgets, subject matter of research, and compensation.

7. *American Demographics* magazine, published monthly by American Demographics, Inc. For subscription information, call 800-365-0688. A readable magazine about demographics—lots of interesting statistics and forecasts.

8. *Congressional Activities* newsletter, published by Oliphant Washington News Service. Provides a summary of coming congressional events such as hearings. Focuses on the energy industry. Available on News-Net.

9. *Congressional Research Report*, published by Penny Hill Press. Provides abstracts of reports published by a research arm of Congress—the Congressional Research Service. Available on NewsNet.

10. Bureau of National Affairs, Inc., 1231 25th Street, NW, Washington, DC 20037; 800-372-1033. Publisher of many reports covering government activities. They include the *United States Law Week; Patent, Copyright and Trademark Journal; Daily Tax Report;* and *Federal Contracts Reporter.* Many BNA reports are available on LEXIS-NEXIS and DIALOG.

11. Claritas, Inc., is a marketing information and demographics data company formed from the merger of Claritas and National Planning Data Corporation (NPDC). They provide information in areas including consumer demographics, market segmentation, consumer expenditures, health care, media, and bank/financial information. Call them at 800-284-4868.

2 | *Secondary Marketing Research: What Information Do You Need?*

This chapter presents a typical marketing plan and shows you how to use it to define research needs. The chapter discusses the types of information obtained by secondary marketing research. It emphasizes the necessity of planning in cost-effective marketing research.

The Marketing Plan

Marketing starts with the creation of a marketing plan. Here is an outline of a typical marketing plan (the sections that are underlined are discussed in this chapter):

I. Title Page
II. Background
    A. Business summary
    B. Market overview
    C. Objectives
III. Marketing Research
    A. Market description and segmentation
    B. Market trends
    C. Competitor assessment
    D. Statistics, customer characteristics, and demographics
    E. Opportunities
    F. Assessment of market risk
IV. Marketing
    A. Statement of unique selling proposition (differentiation)

B. Specific goals
C. Positioning strategy
   1. Overall
   2. Individual products
D. Sales plan
E. Sales promotion plan
V. Communications
   A. Advertising
   B. Public relations
   C. Other (direct mail, telemarketing, etc.)
VI. Implementation
   A. Schedules
   B. Milestones and performance measurement
   C. Reviews and updates

References listed in "For Further Reading" in Chapter 1 and in this chapter discuss the details of the market plan. Cost-effective marketing research requires planning. This point cannot be made too strongly. Your plan defines the information you need and the resources to perform the research. This book covers the marketing research portion of the marketing plan—specifically secondary marketing research and using online sources for that secondary research.

Objectives

Define your objectives and the information you need for cost-effective marketing research. Marketing research can explore the following:

- Basic goals of the company (Determining the viability of basic goals is important for a new company and, periodically, for any company.)
- Products or services that support those goals

- New products or services
- Market environments
- Market share needed to achieve satisfactory profit and return on investment
- Pricing strategies
- Competitors and existing products and services
- Forecasts of potential customer demand
- Distribution channels
- Promotional strategies
- Risk analysis (Anticipate problems and plan responses.)

The objectives of marketing research may be very broad for a new company or for a new product line. Objectives can be very narrow for a product change or for reviewing a new competitor. Save a great deal of time and expense by answering the simple question "What are we trying to accomplish?"

Define the objectives, including the time and budget available to accomplish the task. Time and budget will strongly influence your choice of methodology and choice of information resources. The types of information to be researched are described in the next sections. Knowing the type of information available will assist in the planning process.

Market Description and Segmentation

Markets are the places where goods are bought and sold—where your products or services will be purchased. Use market research to describe markets in terms of the following:

- **Measurability.** How easy it is to determine key market parameters such as customer descriptions. Knowledge of this will help determine the cost of primary marketing research.

- **Accessibility.** How easily you can market and deliver the product. This includes barriers to entry such as entrenched competitors, high delivery costs, and so on.
- **Profitability.** Market size. It must be big enough to make money.
- **Stability.** Technical, political, temporal, and so forth. For example, fads are markets that are temporally unstable.
- **Type of customer.** Consumer, industrial, business, foreign, institutional, or government (or a combination). Although the same product may be sold to all these customers, the marketing is very different depending on customer type.

Markets are segmented into groups (segments) using various descriptions, such as the following:

- **Demographic criteria.** Consumer age, income, leisure activities, and so on.
- **Geographic criteria.** Region, climate, and so on.
- **Psychological criteria.** Consumer traits, company philosophy, and so on.
- **Benefit to customer criteria.** Status, durability, efficiency, reliability, and so on.

Market research can determine these criteria for products, customers, and markets. All of this information affects the market plan: use it to create a market profile that targets customers and their characteristics.

Market Trends

The March 1995 issue of *American Demographics* magazine said that households headed by persons age sixty-five and older will increase by about 20 percent from 1995 to 2010. Is this information interesting to a company developing a magazine for senior citizens? A start-up company may have several years before that great new mousetrap will be available for sale: projections of mouse and cat populations are important. Satisfactory estimates of trends affecting your proposed product are an extremely important part of marketing research.

Trend analysis requires consideration of many factors. The researcher must identify relevant economic issues, technology trends, potential social changes, and projections for natural environments. Estimates must be made of industry size, now and in the future. Both present and future competitors must be identified and analyzed. Competitor forecasts should include growth projections and potential responses to competition.

Forecasting market trends is one of the most difficult tasks in marketing research. It is frequently one of the final research efforts undertaken. Collect all available data before creating forecasts. Industry experts or associations frequently publish forecasts that are good starting points for your own. In addition, data to perform a forecast (such as population growth, geographic movements, and technology changes) is available. If you are interested in a specific new technology, obtain information on the research efforts of leading scientists in that technology. If you are in the housing business, contact the IRS to obtain county growth changes. Define suitable elements in the marketing research plan so that forecasting data can be obtained.

Competitor Assessment

Competitor information is a very good application for secondary marketing research. There is a wealth of publicly available information online about companies. Such information includes financial data, news, and detailed company or industry studies. A useful first step for competitor studies is to group companies by kind of business and study all companies in your line of business.

Define the industry of interest as companies serving the same market. This can be restricted by product or service, distribution channel (all wholesale, for example), or geography. To perform an industry analysis, describe the size, growth, and structure of the industry. Outline the industry marketing practices such as target markets, marketing objectives, and marketing mix.

A common method of classifying businesses or industries by type is the 1987 Standard Industrial Classification System, commonly referred to as the SIC code. It was developed by the U.S. government in conjunction with U.S. businesses. Many databases use the SIC number as an index. It divides virtually all economic activity into divisions, which are further broken up into numbered major groups:

Agriculture, forestry, and fishing	01–09
Mining	10–14
Construction	15–17
Manufacturing	20–39
Transportation, communication, electric, gas, sanitary services	40–49
Wholesale trade	50–51
Retail trade	52–59
Finance, insurance, and real estate	60–67
Services	70–89
Public administration	91–97
Nonclassifiable establishments	99

The SIC places each line of business within one of these ten divisions and assigns it a four-digit code. The first two digits broadly describe the nature of the activity; the third and fourth digits describe the activity quite specifically. There are limits to the system—not all databases categorize companies the same way. Some database vendors, such as Dun & Bradstreet, provide more-detailed systems. D&B adds four more digits to the SIC system, for better differentiation of industry type. International codes are also different.

If there are many current or potential competitors, the best approach is to provide an industry analysis supplemented with data about the most important competitors. If there are only a few competitors, the best approach is to provide a detailed analysis of each competitor.

A corporate profile is a powerful tool for organizing information about competitors. Online systems provide efficient access to data about companies. Develop a corporate profile of your competitor by doing the following:

- Find basic company information from directories. (A frequently used file for this is Dun's Market Identifiers from Dun & Bradstreet.)
- Get the latest *Wall Street Journal, Forbes, Fortune,* or other periodical. (Newspaper and Periodical Abstracts)
- Obtain financial information—for a publicly traded company, look up the annual report. (SEC Online)
- Determine the corporate structure. Who owns them? Who do they own? Who are their subsidiaries? (Corporate Affiliations)
- Get biographical information and news reports on upper management. (Standard & Poor's Register—Biographical)
- Review their products and determine market share. (Trade and Industry Database)
- Review patent holdings and trademarks. (Derwent World Patents Index and TRADEMARKSCAN)
- Read the latest investment analysts' reports. Find out what other people think of your competition. (Investext)

The corporate profile should include company objectives, market position, sales trends, management capabilities, and company strategies. (The subset of market research that focuses on your competitors is called competitor intelligence.)

The files mentioned are located on DIALOG and are shown in Chapter 7. An example of a corporate profile appears in Chapter 8.

Statistics, Customer Characteristics, and Demographics

Consumers are commonly described by various segments: geographics, demographics, and psychographics. Geographics describe where people live. Demographics are the statistics of an area's population, such as number of households and their composition, income, sex, age, education, and occupation. Psychographics in marketing research is the description of people in terms of their personality characteristics and their interests and lifestyles as a reflection of these characteristics.

The U.S. Census is the place to start for consumer data. It provides details about consumers, such as age, sex, ethnicity, size and nature of the living unit, type of dwelling, and rental or value of the dwelling unit. Table 2-1 is an example of data from the Census.

Table 2-1
An Example of Valuable Census Data (From Table 47, 1994 *Statistical Abstract*)

Age Group and Sex	1980 (Number × 1000)	2000 Projection (Number × 1000)
65 and older	25,550	35,322
Males, 65 and older	10,305	14,603
Females, 65 and older	15,245	20,719

In addition to consumer data, the government provides statistics on many subjects. The titles of some tables found in the *1994 Statistical Abstract of the United States*—an invaluable reference that all researchers should own (see

"For Further Reading")—offer an overview of the types of information available.

- Microcomputer Software Sales: 1993 by Application
- Cable and Pay TV—Summary: 1970 to 1993
- National Health Expenditures: 1960 to 1991
- Technology in Public Schools: 1992 and 1993
- Federal Civil Employment—Summary: 1980 to 1992
- Commercial Space Revenues: 1990 to 1994

Opportunities

Marketing research provides knowledge that defines opportunities for selling a product or service. You can determine barriers to entry (such as established competitors or high costs), discover underserved or niche markets, or find new markets created by technological advances. You can research costs for advertising, transportation, or warranty expectations. You can discover how rapidly products are developing in order to correctly budget research and development costs.

New markets created by technological advances are a good example. The invention of the VCR created the opportunity for the video rental industry. An inexpensive and safe transportation system to low Earth orbit would create many new opportunities, such as tourism and microgravity manufacturing.

Assessment of Market Risk

An important part of marketing research is risk appraisal. You must research issues such as the probability of new competition, the potential for major regulatory changes, the possibility of a technological breakthrough, or the chance of major economic change. Define the important risks. Then, make plans to reduce or eliminate the potential impacts on your market. Table 2-2 is an example of a risk matrix that might be generated for a new high-technology product.

Table 2-2
A Sample Risk
Assessment Matrix

Risk Item	Probability of Occurring*	Impact on Market*	Support Research	Response†
Major regulatory change			Monitor key regulations and government activity	
Major economic change			Track economic indicators	
New competitor			Track competitor's investments, technologies, product announcements, etc.	
Alternate technology			Monitor patents and technology	

* Estimate impacts—low, medium, high, or numerical scoring—to determine resource allocation. For example, a high probability of occurrence combined with an estimate of high market impact would demand attention.
† Strategies to minimize the impact of risks are determined by research and planning.

Risk reduction techniques for dealing with a new competitor might include creating higher barriers to entry by spending more on advertising or lowering prices. Another example is developing alternate suppliers to avoid dependence on a single supplier. Risk assessment and mitigation are an important part of a marketing plan. Marketing research identifies the risks and discovers the alternatives. Risk management is a specialty in its own right. Some selected references for this topic are provided at the end of this chapter.

Summary

Planning is necessary for cost-effective marketing research. Without a clear goal, research can be a never ending task. This chapter has presented a typical marketing plan and has discussed the types and applications of information obtained through marketing research.

For Further Reading

1. *Standard Industrial Classification Manual 1987.* Prepared by the Executive Office of the President, Office of Management and Budget. Available through the National Technical Information Service (NTIS) and government bookstores. You must have a copy of this book to perform business searching effectively.

2. *Marketing,* by Robert D. Hisrich (Barron's Business Library, 1990). A concise reference that is extremely useful. Part of a valuable series of business reference books that also includes *Banking, Business Law,* and *Financial and Business Statements.*

3. *State-of-the-Art Marketing Research,* by George Breen and A. B. Blankenship (NTC Business Books, 1993; available through the American Marketing Association). *This is the basic reference to marketing.* If you buy only one book on marketing research, this should be it. It is also available on CD-ROM—as Allegro Reference Series *Business Library Volume 1.*

4. *Statistical Abstract of the United States 1994* (Bureau of the Census; available at government bookstores). Another must-have reference. My starting point for all statistical questions. Fun to look through, also.

Since risk management is a specialized area, I have provided some general references on the subject.

5. "Harvard Study Upends Risk Management Basics," by David M. Katz, *National Underwriter* 98, no. 29 (July 1994): pp. 3, 38.

6. "Project Schedule Risk Assessment," by David T. Hulett, *Project Management Journal* 26, no. 1 (March 1995): pp. 21–31.

7. "Usage and Benefits of Project Risk Analysis and Management," by Steve J. Simister, *International Journal of Project Management* 12, no. 1 (February 1994): pp. 5–8.

8. "Scientific Risk Assessment," *Pesticide & Toxic Chemical News* (December 1, 1993) ISSN: 0146-0501.

9. "Risk Management Software," *ENR* 232, no. 25 (June 1994): p. 65.

10. "Integration of Technical, Cost, and Schedule Risks in Project Management," Jeffrey L. Riggs, Sheila B. Brown, Robert P. Trueblood, *Computers and Operations Research* 21, no. 5 (May 1994): p. 521.

11. "Assessing Marketing Risk," Victor J. Cook Jr., John R. Page, *Journal of Business Research* 15, no. 6 (December 1987): p. 519.

3 | *Where Can You Get Secondary Marketing Research?*

In this chapter, I discuss the broad range of sources available for secondary marketing research and then compare them. At this point, you have created a plan and have defined your information needs. You know the time and budget available. You know the answer to the question "What are we trying to accomplish?"

You can now search for promising information by title, source, or content. Then you select and obtain the desired published material.

Searching can be done in different formats and in different sources. Two important classes of material are the following:

- Online information is material from a computer database, either on-screen or in hard copy (a printout).
- Print information is material that is in print form (such as books and periodicals). It is also microfilm, microfiche, CD-ROM, and slides.

Searching online sources is faster than searching print sources. Online sources can also provide more complete and up-to-date information. However, these computer sources cost money and their use requires skill. An unskilled searcher can waste very large amounts of money online. There is also a trade-off between time and money: if you want it faster, it costs more.

You can do your own searching. If you do lack the time or the appropriate skills, you can hire an information professional or research company to search for you. Communication is very important if you hire research support. The project will proceed smoothly only if everyone involved understands the project. Mistakes are costly, and you can end up acquiring expensive, useless information.

Online Databases Can Be the Most Cost-Effective Sources

Online database vendors and services are the fastest growing sources of data. They provide speed, depth of coverage, and an excellent historical perspective. Most print sources are available in a database. There are more than 5000 databases, covering a complete range of topics and interests. Knight-Ridder, just one of the major professional database publishers, provides more than 450 databases on their DIALOG online service. Database publishers (also called database vendors or online services) create databases from information supplied by database providers (or suppliers) and provide access through an online search system.

Databases cover business, news, law, government, technology of all kinds, intellectual property (patents and copyrights), and general reference (encyclopedias, dictionaries, and so on). Formats include the following:

- **Bibliographical.** These databases generally include the title, the author's name, the journal name, the publication date, and an abstract.

- **Directory.** These databases provide lists such as directories, handbooks, project descriptions, or listings of available grants.

- **Full text.** These are databases that contain the full text of articles.

According to Tim Powell in the February 28, 1994, issue of *Marketing News,* "Information technologies will revolutionize many aspects of marketing and sales during the 1990s." Because marketing (particularly research) is one of the most information-intensive functions in business, it is greatly affected by changes in the information marketplace. Online databases have already made large changes in secondary research in the last ten years.

If used properly, online searching is the most cost-effective research method, particularly if time is a factor. Online searching provides

- the most up-to-date information,
- the most complete information, and
- the fastest results.

> I compare the characteristics and usefulness of the various online sources in Chapter 4. Details of the sources are located in Chapters 6 through 14.

Information Specialists

Information specialists (also called information brokers, information intermediaries, or information consultants) offer secondary marketing research support. In some cases, the specialist may be the reference librarian at a local library that has online database access. In most cases, information specialists are independent businesses. These experts have learned the skills necessary for cost-effective research. They are familiar with the best sources and the latest search techniques.

Information brokers have access to the important online databases and frequently have specific expertise in areas such as chemistry, high technology, international markets, or intellectual property. They frequently have special access to libraries for printed material. They do a great deal of secondary marketing research. Using information brokers is the most cost-effective way of performing small to medium-size secondary marketing research projects: you do not pay the overhead for database access and training and you do not tie up your own key personnel.

Marketing research projects performed by information specialists have included the following:

- Describing opportunities created by government outsourcing.
- Helping a garden supply company to enter new consumer markets.
- Developing the market strategy for a company selling corporate 800 telephone accounts.
- Defining markets, insurance issues, and competitors for a company importing auto security systems.
- Providing distributor and competitor information for a Korean company entering the worldwide personal computer market.
- Providing preliminary market reports for companies interested in selling in Japan. These reports help the companies to decide whether to enter the Japanese market and how much to invest when entering that market.
- Researching business failures and personnel injuries caused by faulty computer software.
- Determining the patents held by a competitor.

> More about information brokers is available from the references at the end of this chapter and at the end of Chapter 4.

Libraries

Libraries are the most cost-effective source for printed material, particularly if you live in a major metropolitan area or near a university. For information too old to be online, libraries are the only source. Many libraries now also have CD-ROM material and access to some online resources. Libraries include the community or public library, the college or university library, and the special library. Special libraries are usually privately maintained by a business or an association and have considerable depth of material for a specialized topic, such as advertising or biotechnology. Useful starting points in a library are guides and reference books such as these:

- *Readers' Guide to Periodical Literature.* A listing of articles in some 200 major periodicals (magazines and journals), classified by topic.
- *Business Periodicals Index.* An index of some 400 business periodicals.
- *Ulrich's International Periodicals Directory.* A directory of periodicals throughout the world.
- *Directory of Corporate Affiliations.* A listing of how companies are interrelated.
- *Wall Street Journal Index.* Business and financial stories published in that publication.
- *New York Times Index.* Abstracts of news items, listed chronologically by subject.
- *Trade Names Dictionary.* A collection of more than 100,000 trade names.
- *Bowker's Books in Print.* A listing of books in print, indexed by author, topic, and publisher.
- *Marquis Who's Who.* Many different directories containing short biographies of important people.
- *Ward's Business Directory of U.S. Private and Public Companies.*
- *Standard & Poor's Register of Corporations, Directors and Executives.*
- *The Corporate Directory of U.S. Public Companies.*

Even if you plan to do online searching, these guides are helpful places to begin. An information professional will probably have one or more of them in his or her office bookcase. The disadvantage of using libraries is time: desired resources may not be available or may be checked out, or you may spend time in a long line at the copy machine.

Libraries are becoming widely available online as well. Local and university library catalogs are available online. The Library of Congress is an expanding resource providing over 26 million records accessible online. The Library of Congress Information System includes federal legislation, Latin American Law, copyright files, organization information, and the catalog.

Market Research Firms

There are many firms listed as market research firms (SIC Code 8732), such as Information Resources, MARC, and Mediamark Research (MRI). Some market research firms will perform secondary research as a separate task or they will do it as part of an entire research project. Most large firms emphasize primary research. The types of research firms and what they offer (mostly for primary research) are outlined here:

- Firms selling custom-designed studies. They perform a study specifically for your project. This can be very expensive. Market research firms may provide one or more of the specialized tasks listed below. Some firms specialize in one or more areas. Few firms can do all tasks well.

  —Mail surveys.

  —Personal interview studies.

  —Telephone studies.

  —Panels.

—Secondary research.

—Sampling.

—Focus groups.

—In addition, there are research firms that specialize in problems of segmentation, customer databases, or advertising studies.

- Firms selling standardized studies. These can be firms that perform large consumer statistical studies (like Nielsen) or firms like Find/SVP that provide prepackaged studies on specific topics. A typical example is a report called *The Household Insecticide Market* (Find/SVP, November 1994, 100+ pages, $1850). These reports are expensive, but they are cheaper than full custom reports because they are sold to multiple buyers. However, these standardized studies can go out of date quickly. Also, no report may be available for your specific application.

- Firms selling software, survey samples, and so on. There are many vendors of market-related software or forms. ZIP code software, mapping software, automated statistical analysis programs, and survey preparation software are examples. These programs may help lower your overall marketing costs.

- Firms selling mailing lists or market databases. If all you need is access to specific customer groups segmented in various ways, there are many firms providing this type of service. If your project is large enough (about a 1000-name mailing list, for example), this can be a cost-effective approach for part of a research project.

Interviews, Polls, Focus Groups, or Experts

Interviews, polls, and focus groups are important methods in primary marketing research. Many books cover such topics. Results from applicable previous studies should be reviewed as part of any secondary research project.

Interviews with industry or technology experts can provide very valuable added information for secondary marketing research. Therefore, a comprehensive secondary research program should call on experts. For example, I discovered an article in a journal that was important to my client's marketing plans. By calling the author of the article, I obtained information that significantly changed the results. In another case, I could not find a critical piece of information. By contacting an expert in the technology, I was told about a new report that would not be published for a year!

> Remember: the most up-to-date information is in someone's head!

Trade Associations and Other Sources

Trade, business, or professional associations are another good possibility for business and professional markets. These associations provide access to experts and to literature published by the association. Listings of these associations can be found in the library or in the references at the end of this chapter.

The federal government is also a source of massive amounts of information. For example, the Census is the largest single source of secondary data in this country. Population, jobs, and industries are only a few of the subjects included. The following categories and examples show the range of data available from the Bureau of the Census:

- **Agriculture.** The number and sizes of farms in each state.
- **Business.** The number of firms, employees, and payroll by industry.
- **Construction and housing.** Price and cost indices for construction.

- **Foreign trade.** U.S. exports and imports of merchandise.
- **Government.** State and local government retirement systems.
- **International.** Population by country.
- **Manufacturing.** Summaries by industry and year.
- **Population.** Population projections to 2050.
- **Genealogy and age.** Marriage status by age.

> An example of the Census data available on the Internet is shown in Chapter 11.

Other general sources include local government—state, county, and municipal. But local government sources have not been very helpful in the past: the data has been limited, restricted by law, out of date, or inaccurate. As governments move further into the electronic age, these sources will improve.

Local or regional chambers of commerce are definitely worth calling. Although their helpfulness has varied greatly, some chambers have been very good sources.

CD-ROMs

A rapidly advancing area of information access is the use of CD-ROMs. Many libraries and businesses have installed CD-ROM databases, such as newspaper and periodical indexes. Most personal computers are now being delivered with CD-ROM drives installed, creating a large area for growth. A Gallup poll shows that almost all Fortune 1000 companies and 73 percent of small-to-midsize companies employ CD-ROM drives. Worldwide shipments of CD-ROM drives were expected to reach 17.45 million units in 1994, a 160 percent increase over 1993; a further increase to 23 million units is expected by 1996. Companies are now using CD-ROMs to store their technical manuals and databases. The CD-ROM drive market is being pushed by the accelerating number of available CD-ROM products.

Inexpensive titles (less than $200) include dictionaries, encyclopedias, business books, company directories, and phone books. Pro CD offers a set of SelectPhone CD-ROMs that contains phone numbers culled from the white pages of all the phone books in the United States. DeLorme Mapping's *Street Atlas USA 2.0* provides users with displays varying from small neighborhoods to the whole country; on this CD, users can search by phone number, street name, ZIP code, and city.

Another useful, inexpensive title is *Hoover's Multimedia Business 500* (listed at $49.95), from the Reference Press. *Business 500* gives you *Hoover's Handbook of Business 1995* on CD-ROM, which offers comprehensive and up-to-date information on 500 major U.S. companies, public and private. You can search through this database quickly and easily and extract the information you need into your word processor.

Business Library Volume 1, from Allegro New Media (with special thanks to NTC Publishing Group and Prentice-Hall, Inc.) gives you the complete text of twelve popular books, all written by well-known experts in major business fields. Some of the books included are these:

- *Business to Business Communications Handbook*, by Fred R. Messer
- *Finance and Accounting for Nonfinancial Managers*, by Steven A. Finkler
- *State-of-the-Art Marketing Research*, by A. B. Blankenship and George Edward Breen
- *Successful Direct Marketing Methods*, by Bob Stone

More expensive titles (up to several thousand dollars) are also available. Suppliers include the U.S. government and major publishers. Knight-Ridder, for example, publishes more than sixty titles, such as *KR Information On Disk Corporate America.* The National Technical Information Service (NTIS) publishes titles such as the *National Trade Data Bank* and *Planetary Images.* Another major supplier, Gale Research, provides more than thirty databases on CD-ROM, including the *Encyclopedia of Associations* and *Fast Reference Facts.*

One big advantage of CD-ROMs is that the cost is defined. For a single purchase or subscription price, unlimited searches can be run. They are an excellent choice if many searches on the contained material will be performed. The disadvantages include the following:

- **Timeliness.** Depending on the subscription, updates may be available every second month, every quarter, or less frequently. Information is also delayed by the manufacturing time of the discs. They must be supplemented with other sources to include the latest information.

- **Cost.** The combined cost of the computer, CD-ROM drive(s), and the CD adds up to a large investment. It is too large an outlay for infrequent use.

- **Search tools.** Although the data available has grown dramatically, not all CD-ROMs have good software to help you find what you need. Some are much harder to use than the equivalent print resource.

Summary

The various sources of information for secondary marketing research have been briefly reviewed. All sources have advantages and disadvantages: any one may be the best for a specific task. For the real best choice, use an expert, who will select the best combination of sources. Using information brokers is the most cost-effective way of performing small to medium-size secondary marketing research projects. You do not pay the overhead for database access and training, and you do not tie up key internal personnel.

Table 3-1 summarizes the sources and their characteristics.

Table 3-1
The Characteristics of Information Resources— From the Library to the Online World

Source	Cost	Timeliness	Speed
Online	Low to medium—but can be high if incorrectly used	Excellent	Excellent
Information specialists	Low to medium	Excellent	Excellent
Libraries	Low	Good to excellent	Good
Market research firms	High	Excellent	Good
Interviews, focus groups, and others	Medium to high, depending on size	Excellent	Fair
Trade associations and other sources	Low	Poor to excellent	Fair to good
CD-ROMs	High initial and low recurring	Poor to good	Good to excellent

For Further Reading

1. *CD-ROMs and Optical Disks Available from NTIS* (National Technical Information Service, Catalog PR-888, 703-487-4650). A good (and growing) list of CD-ROMs, it includes discs on defense, trade, health, speech recognition, and economics.

2. *CD-ROM Professional* is a magazine published by Pemberton Press that provides CD-ROM information for the professional user. It is a well-written magazine that should be on your list if you are or will be using CD-ROMs. For subscription information, call 800-222-3766, ext. 517. (In Connecticut, call 203-761-1466, ext. 517.)

3. The Association of Independent Information Professionals. The professional organization for information brokers. For more information on information specialists, contact AIIP Headquarters, 245 Fifth Avenue,

Suite 2103, New York, NY 10016; 212-779-1855, 212-481-3071 (fax), CompuServe 73263,34.

4. *Burwell World Directory of Information Brokers,* edited by Helen P. Burwell and published annually by Burwell Enterprises, Inc., 3724 F.M. 1960 W., Suite 214, Houston, TX 77068; 713-537-9051. This comprehensive directory provides information about experts in the art and science of information retrieval. With over 1800 entries from more than forty-five countries in the 1995 edition, it is a great resource to find expert help. You can search by location, by foreign expertise, by subject specialties, or by services provided.

5. *Business Information Sources,* Third Edition, by Lorna M. Daniells (University of California Press, 1993). This is a guide to business books and business sources prepared by the retired head of the reference department at the Harvard Business School Baker Library. A necessity for marketing research. The book covers all business topics, including

   • U.S. business and economic trends

   • Industry statistics

   • Management

   • Investment sources

   • Marketing

6. *Who Knows What,* by Daniel Starer (Henry Holt Reference Books, 1992). Another good reference for locating information sources. It is organized as an alphabetical directory, with each section listing applicable associations, periodicals, libraries, companies, and government sources. In the marketing area, there are sections on advertising, consumers, direct mail, marketing, market research, and telemarketing. A good starting point for locating experts, it even has a section called "How to Get Information by Telephone."

7. *The Information Please Business Almanac and Source Book 1995,* edited by Seth Godin (Houghton Mifflin). Another useful reference, with listings of more than 4000 associations, organizations, companies, and government agencies. This book provides area codes, ZIP codes, shipping rates, city maps, media contacts, 800 telephone numbers, and more. Another book that is fun to read.

8. *The Information Catalog,* published by Find/SVP, 625 Avenue of the Americas, New York, NY 10011; 800-346-3787. This is a catalog of industry and market research reports and Wall Street reports. It also includes books, documents, and software for marketing and marketing research.

9. SilverPlatter Information, Inc., is a major publisher of professional CD-ROM databases. For more information, call 800-343-0064 or write to SilverPlatter, 100 River Ridge Drive, Norwood, MA 01262-5043.

10. The Reference Press is the publisher or distributor of many reasonably priced reference products, including *Hoover's Handbook of American Business*. Contact them at 800-486-8666 or 6448 Highway 290 East, Suite E-104, Austin, TX 78723.

11. *Encyclopedia of Associations* describes more than 23,000 associations and includes contact information. It is available in hard copy or CD-ROM from Gale Research, P.O. Box 33477, Detroit, MI 48232-5477; 800-877-4253. You can also request a catalog listing all of the many information products from Gale Research.

Additional Sources

Besides the sources that I use regularly that I just listed, there are many other useful sources. (These may be accessed via online, CD-ROM, or at a library.) Some of these sources include the following:

- *Moody's Manuals*—The definitive sources of histories of public companies (800-342-5647).
- *Standard & Poor's Sheets* and *The Standard & Poor's Stock Guide*—Quick references on publicly held companies (800-221-5277).
- *Dun & Bradstreet*—The nation's largest provider of credit information on companies, including small and private ones (800-365-3867). *The Business Information Report* (BIR) is a very useful D&B product (800-223-1026).
- *The Value Line Investment Survey*—Quarterly updates on 1700 publicly held companies (800-833-0046).
- Company public relations departments or investor relations departments.
- Disclosure, Inc., provides SEC documentation in printed and electronic form (800-638-8241).
- Business periodicals:
  —*Wall Street Journal*
  —*Forbes*
  —*Fortune*
  —*Business Week*
  —*The Economist*, published in the United Kingdom
  —*Financial Times*, the United Kingdom's equivalent to the *Wall Street Journal*

—*Investors Daily, Inc.*

—*Financial World*

- Directories available on specific industries and topics:

  —*Best's Insurance Reports*

  —*Polk's Bank Directory*

  —CorpTech's *Corporate Technology Directory*

  —*International Directory of Company Histories* (eleven volumes), Gale Research (800-877-4253)

4 | *Online Sources for Secondary Marketing Research*

This chapter summarizes the many sources of online data for marketing research and presents their characteristics. Providing information is a big business. It requires a great deal of effort for a researcher to stay current. A researcher selects the correct information sources by comparing the different source features with his or her needs. Important characteristics include

- Reasonable cost.
- Market focus. Does the source cover the areas of interest to a marketing researcher: a business source instead of a scientific source?
- Information available, including geographic coverage for the parts of the world where you want to sell.
- User-friendly interface.
- Power and ease of use of search tools.
- Data quality or accuracy. The database has very few typographic errors and accurately represents the original source.
- User support. Do they answer the phone? Do they answer questions now? Are their answers correct?

Many sources can be used for information research. I divide those sources into three broad categories that are differentiated by interface, market, information coverage, cost, and search tools.

First are the professional sources. These are characterized by an in-depth coverage of topics and by their primary marketplace of professional and business users. Sources in this group include Dow Jones, DIALOG, and LEXIS-NEXIS. These are the best choice for the secondary marketing researcher.

Second is the Internet. (Although bulletin board systems are not the Internet, they share important characteristics with the Internet from a researcher's view. They will not be discussed further.) The Internet is characterized by its breadth and eclectic nature.

Last are the consumer services, such as America Online (AOL) and CompuServe. They are characterized by a broad range of services, including many leisure-time areas. Their primary market is the consumer.

As I cover these sources in detail in the next few chapters, I will look closely at their differences. I will also analyze the impact of the various characteristics on the need for cost-effective secondary marketing research; this will allow you to select the best sources.

Professional Sources

Professional databases are the premier tools for the marketing researcher. They have excellent access, high-quality data, and comprehensive customer support. They have excellent search tools that are continuously improving. Support for the searcher is excellent, including extensive documentation, training classes, and telephone support.

Disadvantages are cost and complexity. The advantages of high-quality data and excellent support do not come cheaply. Professional services may have up-front costs, training costs, documentation costs, or monthly minimums. Charges for hourly connect time may be high, and charges for document output may also be high. However, costs are dropping because of technology and competition.

Interfaces are frequently complex, to accommodate the most accurate search tools. Again, change is here. New natural-language and menu interfaces are making access easier.

For marketing research, doing a timely and satisfactory job of obtaining the right information is vital. The professional services are the lowest-cost option for marketing research.

> Important professional databases and their use are covered in depth in Chapters 6, 7, and 8.

The Internet

The Internet is the online information world to many people, due to the coverage by the popular press. It started small as ARPANET in 1969, supporting government needs and research laboratories. It has grown dramatically since then and today is a major force in the information world. All discussions of online information are held with an awareness of both the reality and the mythology of the Internet. By some estimates the Internet is doubling in size every eight to ten months. It is perhaps already too big to explore efficiently. Technical users describe it as a "network of networks." From a researcher's view, its key features include

- Its large size.
- Its rapid growth and change.
- The breadth of knowledge available.
- Increasing commercial participation—both by access providers and by information providers.
- Its connectivity. It effectively ties in an Internet-connected computer to all other Internet-connected computers. It provides an immense opportunity for information exchange.

However, the Internet has significant weaknesses, including poor search tools, lack of quality control for data, and lack of user support. It is difficult to use effectively. According to Elisabeth Logan (in a paper presented at the 1995 National Online Conference), professional services were significantly better for finding information. Internet searches were slower and less useful.

The Internet has growing pains—the culture is changing and bandwidth problems frequently occur (forcing users to wait what seems like forever for data transfer). Size is both a weakness and a strength.

Dealing with and understanding the information available via the Internet is necessary for the information professional and will be increasingly useful to the secondary marketing researcher.

> I discuss the cost-effective use of the Internet for secondary marketing research in Chapters 9, 10, and 11.

Consumer Sources

Consumer sources are used mostly by consumers at home. These services are not designed for professional use. However, there is an ever-increasing amount of valuable information on such services. In addition, CompuServe, America Online, Prodigy, and others provide access (called gateways) to professional services and to the Internet. Advantages include relatively low cost, easy access, and a broad range of information. Disadvantages include weak search tools and incomplete information. For example, on CompuServe, I can view the latest issues of *Fortune,* but I cannot search the last ten years of *Fortune.*

If you search infrequently, the consumer sources are useful. You can obtain a great deal of information by using what is available directly or by using the gateways to other services. By using the gateways, short-term access to DIALOG and other professional services is available without paying yearly costs or adding an expensive connection. For longer-term access, the gateways are very expensive.

> Chapters 12, 13, and 14 provide details and examples for the consumer sources.

Summary

In this chapter, I have introduced the three primary types of online sources for use in secondary marketing research: professional sources, the Internet, and consumer sources. I believe the professional services are the best choice for marketing or professional searchers. Table 4-1 is a summary of their characteristics.

Table 4-1   A Comparison of Online Sources—Professional Services Are the Best Choice

	Cost	Information	Search Tools	Data Quality	User Support
Internet	Low to high	Broad, not complete	Weak but evolving	Variable—no quality control	Limited
Professional	High	Most complete	Excellent and getting better	Very good	Excellent
Consumer	Medium	Good	Weak	Good	Good

For Further Reading

1. *The Internet Challenge,* a paper presented by Elisabeth Logan of Florida State University at the National Online Conference, 1995. This paper shows interesting comparisons of searching done by advanced students using the Internet and professional services. Searches on the Internet were 74 percent useful and slow, compared to a 95 percent useful estimate for searches on professional services.

2. *Information for Sale,* second edition, by John H. Everett and Elizabeth P. Crowe (Windcrest/McGraw-Hill, 1994). This book is written for the aspiring information broker. It has a great list of books, articles, seminars, directories, CD-ROM publishers, online services, magazines, newsletters, and professional associations.

3. *The Information Broker's Handbook,* second edition, by Sue Rugge and Alfred Glossbrenner (Windcrest/McGraw-Hill, 1995). The best book for the beginning information broker, with a very professional approach. It is also a good book to read for a background on the information business.

4. *The Whole Earth Online Almanac: Info from A to Z,* by Don Rittner (Brady, 1993). A good general survey of the Internet, consumer services, bulletin boards, a few professional services, and CD-ROMs. The majority of the book is an alphabetical listing of topics with appropriate sources.

5. *PC Communications Bible,* by Jerry Pournelle and Michael Banks (Microsoft Press, 1992). A good overview of the computer part of getting online.

6. *The Electronic Traveler: Exploring Alternative Online Systems,* by Elizabeth P. Crowe (Windcrest/McGraw-Hill, 1994). This book explores access to the Internet, DASnet, NetCom, and many other systems. Good starting place for a beginner.

7. *The Electronic Information Report,* a newsletter published forty-six times a year by Simba Information, Inc. (ISSN: 1076-0490). It provides useful information, statistics, and forecasts for the industry. The subscription is $399 per year (as of this writing). Contact Simba Information, Inc., P.O. Box 7430, Wilton, CT 06897; (203) 834-0033, fax (203) 834-1771.

8. *Gale Directory of Databases,* edited by Kathleen Lopez Nolan. Published every six months by Gale Research, Inc., P.O. Box 33477, Detroit, MI 48232-5477; 800-877-4253. Volume 1 covers online databases, and volume 2 covers CD-ROMs and other "portable" databases.

The standard reference for locating data online. Databases are indexed by name, location, and subject. The January 1995 edition lists 5342 databases, 2202 producers, and 828 online services. It is also available online on DataStar and ORBIT-QUESTAL. You should also get the Gale catalog, as they publish many other useful references.

5 | *Search Skills*

Basic search skills are necessary to use all information sources, not just online sources. Online sources just allow you to waste money faster if you are unprepared. Although each type of information source has a different interface, basic search techniques are common to all sources.

You must invest time to learn these skills if you want to find information within a reasonable time and for an affordable cost. If you are going to do your own online market research, you must develop search skills. Otherwise, hire an expert: you will save time, money, and frustration. Even if you hire an expert, a basic understanding of the search process will help you communicate your task.

Define the Problem

The first step in any search effort is defining the problem. If you do not know what you want, you will not find it. Ask yourself these questions:

1. What are we trying to accomplish?
2. What information do we need to achieve that goal?
3. How much time and money do we have?

For example, while writing this book, I wanted to know how much money was spent on marketing research during the last few years. Therefore, I answered, for myself, the key questions

1. *What am I trying to accomplish?* Learn how much money was spent on marketing research during the last few years.
2. *What information do I need to achieve that goal?* Recent statistics and numbers that specify how much money was spent on primary and secondary marketing research.
3. *How much time and money do I have?* One day and less than $200.

The tight schedule required me to use online sources. Now my problem was defined, and I had enough information to proceed to the next step.

Understand the Vocabulary of Your Problem

The next step is to generate a list of key words and phrases to use as search terms. Spend some time learning the vocabulary of your problem. Use references (such as dictionaries, encyclopedias, textbooks, and handbooks) to help if you are not completely familiar with the research area. A researcher must be comfortable with the specialized language of the field being searched because the authors and indexers of the information you seek will communicate in that language.

Searching itself also has a vocabulary of its own. See the box for some definitions of the more common terms.

Familiarity with international terminology, foreign languages, and alternative spellings is also important to ensure completeness. Even searching for common misspellings can be helpful to pick up all the information.

Searching Has Its Own Technology

abstract: a summary of an article or document.

controlled vocabulary: standardized terms (often called descriptors) used to describe subject content of records in a database. Descriptors give an indication of the content of the article, book, or document.

coverage: geographic regions, topics, or time span included in a database.

database: an electronic collection of single information elements, called records. Also called a file.

database or record format: Includes the following:

- **bibliographic:** databases that contain bibliographic information such as title, publication name, author's name, publication date, and abstract.

- **statistical/numerical:** databases that contain information in numeric-only format.

- **full text:** databases that contain the complete text of articles or other sources.

database producer: an organization that either offers its own information or collects information from other sources and produces it in electronic format.

field: an easily identifiable segment of a database record. Fields can include title, author, journal, publication date, index terms, abstracts, and text.

format: a type of output requested, such as title, full text, bibliographic, or KWIC.

index: an alphanumeric list of words and phrases in a database.

keywords: important words that express the concepts of a search topic.

KWIC: a format option that displays only the part of a record that contains selected search terms. Useful to quickly review the accuracy of results.

menu: a list of options to control a search. Allows searching without learning the details of commands.

proximity: the relative location of selected terms.

record: a complete, single item in a database.

reprint: a copy of the full text of a document obtained through a document delivery service or other means.

SDI: Selective Dissemination of Information. Also called an alert or current awareness. An automatic search repeat at selected intervals to track the most current information.

search terms: words or phrases that describe the subject of interest in a search. Also called keywords.

stop word: a common word in the English language that is normally ignored in a search statement. Examples of stop words are *the, of, a, at, by, for,* and *with.* Also, don't use command words (such as AND and OR).

thesaurus: a list of the controlled vocabulary.

truncation: the process of searching for all words that start with the same letters. Cut off a word after a carefully chosen letter in order to retrieve variant word endings, singular and plural forms of words, and words with the identical root.

In my example search, I used these search terms: *market research, marketing research, cost(s), budget(s), expense(s), expenditure(s), primary,* and *secondary.*

Determine Appropriate Sources for Your Research

Find out what journals or newspapers report on your project area. Find online sources that include those journals or newspapers by using reference books or reference materials provided by database vendors. Select and use sources that cover the topics of your search. In my example, I wanted business references and articles written for professional marketing people, so I chose the following (from DIALOG):

- Databases that cover selected journals, such as *Marketing Management, Marketing News, Marketing Research, Marketing Science, Marketing Times,* and *Marketing Week*

- Databases that are business-oriented or include magazines that cover marketing information

These are the databases I selected:

- Trade & Industry Database, from Information Access Company
- ABI/INFORM, from UMI
- PTS PROMT, from Information Access Company
- Magazine Index, from Information Access Company
- McGraw-Hill Publications Online, from McGraw-Hill
- PTS Newsletter DB, from Information Access Company
- Time Publications, from Time, Inc.
- PTS MARS, from Information Access Company

These databases all met the specified criteria. I searched multiple databases because each covers a different selection of material. Sometimes one can use a single database, but using multiple databases reduces the chance of missing a critical piece of information.

Understand Simple Search Logic

There are simple elements of search logic that are common to many searching systems. If you learn basic Boolean logic commands, along with truncation and proximity commands, you can perform effective searches. The set of software search tools provided by a database vendor is called the command language.

The basic approach (the logic system) used for online searching is Boolean logic. This system was developed by the English mathematician George Boole around 1850 to permit algebraic manipulation of logical statements. When used in online research, Boolean logic creates useful sets of information. Boolean logic uses AND, OR, and NOT connectors (also called operators) between search terms.

The AND connector requires both terms to be present. "A AND B" means the result must contain both A and B. The diagram in Figure 5-1 shows the function of AND. Use AND to link the main terms of your search.

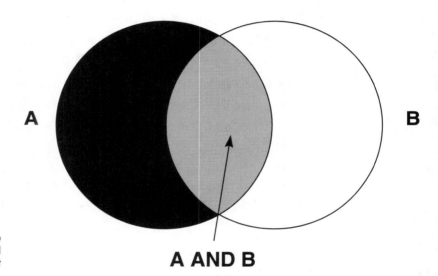

A AND B

Figure 5-1
The Boolean AND function requires all terms to be in the result

The OR connector requires either term to be present. "A OR B" means the result must contain either A or B. Of course, both may be present. The diagram in Figure 5-2 shows how OR functions. Use OR to find synonyms or alternative spellings.

The NOT connector requires a term not to be present. "A NOT B" means the result must contain A but cannot contain B. Figure 5-3 shows the NOT function. Use NOT with caution because it may discard results you actually want. For example, if you wanted articles about cats, but not about cats and dogs, you could specify "cats NOT dogs." Now you would have all articles about cats with no mention of dogs. You would probably miss some very good articles mostly about cats if they mentioned the word *dogs* even once.

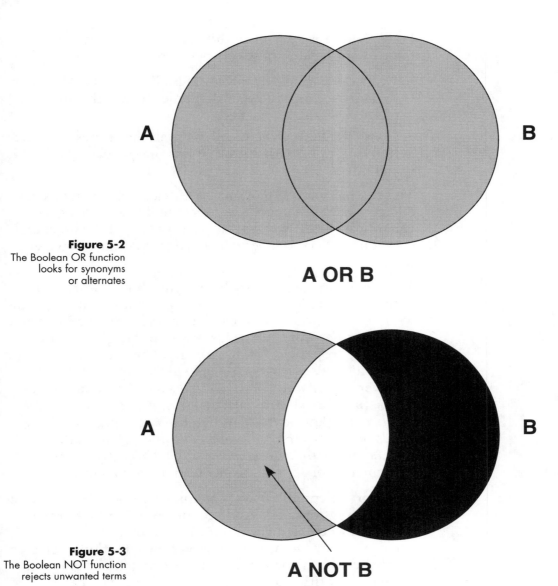

Figure 5-2
The Boolean OR function looks for synonyms or alternates

A OR B

Figure 5-3
The Boolean NOT function rejects unwanted terms

A NOT B

Use parentheses to control the order of operation. Items contained within parentheses are performed first.

- "(cats OR dogs) AND mice" finds all the stories that mention either cats or dogs in the same story with a mention of mice.
- "cats OR (dogs AND mice)" finds all the stories that mention cats along with all the stories that mention both dogs and mice.

This distinction is important because different vendors use different orders of operation. I recommend always using parentheses—that way you are always sure of the order and do not have to remember which database vendor you are using.

The two other common tools that you should be familiar with are truncation and proximity. Truncation (that is, using wild cards) allows you to search easily plurals, spelling variations, or other word variations. For example, if "?" is the wild card, "copyright?" finds *copyright* and *copyrights.* "Wom?n" finds *woman* and *women.* Do not use truncation with very short words. For example, "cat?" finds all words whose first three letters are *cat: cat, cats, cataclysm, catacomb, catafalque, catalepsy, catalog, catalogue, catalpa, catalysis, catalyst, catamaran, catamount, catapult, . . . cataract, catarrh, catastrophe, . . . CATV, catwalk,* and perhaps many more. You probably do not want all of these.

Proximity selection allows searching words or terms in specified relationships. The AND connector will find selected words anywhere in a document. With proximity connectors, you can specify words to be adjacent, near (within a selected number of words), or in the same section of the document (paragraph or title, for example). In addition, you can specify which word comes first. For example, in LEXIS-NEXIS, requesting "market w/1 share" returns *market share* and does not retrieve *share of market.*

Create Your Research Strategy

Using your keyword list and simple logic, prepare your search statements. In my example, I used this search statement:

(MARKET OR MARKETING)(W1)RESEARCH? (S)(PRIMARY AND SECONDARY) (S)(COST? OR BUDGET? OR EXPEN?) /1994-1995

This statement looks for all the articles that mention *market* (or *marketing*) *research* (or *researches* or *researcher* or *researchers*). Those terms must be in the same part of the document with both *primary* and *secondary*. Then, they must also be in the same part of the document with *cost* (or *costs* or *costing*), *budget* (or *budgets* or *budgetary*), and *expense* (or *expenses* or *expenditure* or *expenditures*). Because I was interested in recent articles, I also limited the search to articles from 1994 and 1995. The use of Boolean, truncation, and proximity operators allows you to write very complicated statements in a concise and precise format.

Go Online

Finally, after you are fully prepared, you are ready to go online. Preparation pays dividends—you minimize costs and do not waste time. The example search retrieved seventeen articles, of which the following all had valuable information:

1. "Information Technology Helps Reengineer Research"
2. "The Changing Role of Market Research"
3. "From Online Specialist to Research Manager: Changing with the Times"
4. "Through the Marketing Glass"
5. "Market Research for Your Export Operations: Part I—Using Secondary Sources of Research"

6. "Getting the Most from Research Resources"
7. "Auditing Ourselves"
8. "The Changing Role of Market Research (Part 1)"

Refine the Search

Remember, searching is interactive. In the example, I reviewed the search results by eye and rejected nine of the seventeen. What if I had received a very large number of results that I could not scan quickly? What if I had received no useful results? The next step is to learn from the results and modify the search.

If I had received no useful results, I could have searched additional years or added more databases. The search statement could be modified. For example, I could search on (PRIMARY OR SECONDARY) which would expand the search results. If I had received too many results, I could have limited the search further by requiring that my search terms appear in the titles of documents. Improve your results by modifying your strategy as you go.

Collect and Report Results

Once you have a set of documents that you want, you can get output many different ways, depending on the database and system. Here are some of the things you can do:

1. Download full text (or capture) to your computer—the fastest way. However, most downloaded information is text only: graphs, pictures, and some tables are not available. This situation is improving with the increasing availability of image files that contain all the graphics information as well as the text.

2. Have documents E-mailed, mailed, or faxed to you.

3. Find them in the library.

When you have your documents, it is an excellent practice to place them in a report or folder along with the problem definition, sources used, search logic used, and search results. This practice allows you to learn from previous searches and allows you to reconstruct a search if someone misplaces the delivered documents.

Summary

In the real world, searching is not quite this simple. However, these basic concepts will be part of all successful research efforts. Specific examples of these general guidelines will be shown throughout the following chapters. Some additional suggestions for improving search skills are these:

• Take training from a vendor on how to use online databases. Commercial vendors such as DIALOG provide such instruction. Contact vendors and get their training schedules.

• Check with local colleges or adult education programs for classes on online searching.

• Investigate your local libraries. Many have CD-ROM stations that can provide good search practice.

For Further Reading

1. *How to Look It Up Online: Get the Information Edge with Your Personal Computer*, by Alfred Glossbrenner (St. Martin's Press, 1987). Good book for beginners. Specific examples are out of date, but it remains a useful book with excellent descriptions of the online search process.

2. *Electronic Style: A Guide to Citing Electronic Information,* by Xia Li and Nancy B. Crane (MecklerMedia, 1993). A useful guide to citing results obtained from online databases in your reports.

3. *Secrets of the Super Searchers,* by Reva Basch (Online, Inc./8-Bit Books, 1994). A collection of interviews with very experienced information experts. They offer insights into searching that they learned the hard way. Anyone interested in searching should have this book.

4. *Find It Online!* by Robert I. Berkman (TAB Books, 1994). Another good book to get started.

5. *Online Information Hunting,* by Nahun Goldmann (Windcrest/McGraw-Hill, 1992). The author presents an interesting case that the best searchers are always subject specialists: the best searcher for marketing information would be a marketing expert who has learned searching. The book provides an excellent description of search skills and techniques.

6. *Using Online Scientific and Engineering Data Bases,* by Haley Bjelland (Windcrest/McGraw-Hill, 1992). Another good introduction to the basics of searching. Although the author focuses on scientific and engineering databases, the methodology applies to all searches.

6 | *The Professional Services— Characteristics*

This chapter introduces the professional (sometimes called commercial) databases. These are the premier tools for the marketing researcher. The services range from the major publishers of multiple databases, such as DIALOG from Knight-Ridder and LEXIS-NEXIS from Reed Elsevier, to small publishers that may have only one, very focused database. When doing a timely and satisfactory job of obtaining the right information is vital, the professional services are the lowest-cost option. In this chapter, I look at the general characteristics of professional databases. I also discuss potential problems with using these sources.

What Is a Professional Information Service?

The professional information service is defined by its target market; features, capabilities, and innovation are driven by that market. Therefore, the professional information service is characterized by the following:

- Excellent access
- High-quality data
- Comprehensive data
- Complete customer support, including
  —Extensive documentation.
  —Training classes.
  —Telephone support.

—Powerful command-language search tools that are continuously improving.

—User-friendly communication software. New point-and-click interfaces are very helpful.

In the last few years, professional services have increasingly provided

- More full-text sources
- More images
- Shorter lag times to online availability
- More integrated searches or integrated files—so searches can cover more sources at one time
- Better search tools, including relevancy or natural-language tools

The overall information-access process has become better integrated, with one-stop shopping from search to document delivery.

Who Uses Professional Services?

Well-trained professional searchers are the primary customers of the professional information service. The service's primary market focus is the professional information user who understands and appreciates the value of the information. The vast quantity of information available, combined with the complex search languages, has led to a steep learning curve for efficient use. Therefore, the most frequent users of these services are the trained, professional users of information who have learned efficient searching. Typical users are

- Librarians
- Investors
- Marketing researchers
- Scientists
- Information brokers

However, most of these services are also trying to reach the much larger number of information end users.

Are Professional Services Expensive?

No. The ability to access the best data in the most efficient fashion makes the professional services economical. But the advantages of high-quality data and excellent support do not come cheap: Professional services charge up-front costs, training costs, documentation costs, and/or monthly minimums. Charges for hourly connect time may be high, and charges for document output may also be high. The training of searchers requires a significant time investment, which is also expensive. However, in the near future, increased competition will lower prices, and new search technology will lower training and support costs.

Complexity is another problem. Complex search interfaces, very large numbers of databases, and multiple pricing schemes all exist in order to provide all the tools that allow efficient information retrieval. (These variations also provide market differentiation between vendors.) Search logic and command languages are complicated and vary greatly among vendors.

Even the simple act of picking a database varies. For example, to begin a search on DIALOG, you select the file you want by entering "Begin ###," where "###" is the number of the file you want. On Dow Jones, you type "//nnnn," where "nnnn" is the name of the file you want to access. Other vendors have other methods.

Because search tools are complex (and differ so much between vendors), novices may find themselves incurring significant online costs while retrieving mainly false drops—articles that meet the search criteria but are not truly relevant.

Different vendors have different cost structures. Both the costs and types of costs vary greatly in different systems.

The lowest-cost search techniques will differ on a different system. For example:

- In DIALOG, you typically pay for the time you spend in your selected database plus telecommunication time. You pay a varying fee for output.

- In LEXIS-NEXIS, you typically pay a fixed fee for each search that is not time-dependent, plus telecommunication time. You pay for lines printed.

- In Dow Jones, you typically pay no time charges except telecommunication time. You pay for characters printed.

Costs are not that simple, however. The trained searcher must consider a wide variety of cost elements that make up the final bill, including

- Annual fee, monthly fee, or a monthly minimum.

- Documentation costs.

- Software costs.

- Telecommunication costs—the cost of hooking up to the service each time you are online.

- Hourly or per-minute database fees.

- Output charges. For example, you may be charged per article or you may be charged per character or line printed.

To minimize the bill, you need experience and knowledge of the system. The biggest payoff comes from search preparation: Think Before You Dial!

Search Tools Are Complex and Powerful

Command search interfaces are frequently complex, in order to provide the most accurate search tools. A professional searcher must spend significant effort to be familiar with even one of the systems; the problem is compounded when accessing multiple systems. The only solution is training and study.

Change is coming. New natural-language (covered in the next section) and menu interfaces are making access easier. One way of keeping up is to concentrate on learning one vendor's command interface and use menu interfaces for other vendors. However, menu interfaces and the current generation of natural-language interfaces do not yield the same performance as the command interface.

Boolean tools (combining search terms with operators such as AND, OR, and NOT) are the basis of the search language in all of the various systems. Each database has its own tools or language. Common important features of the search tools include the following:

- The use of truncation or wild cards. For example, if "*" is the wild card, "cat*" searches for all words whose first three letters are *cat*. "Wom*n" finds *woman* and *women*.

- The ability to limit searches by field, such as title or lead paragraph.

- An online or printed thesaurus that lets you look up elements (words, phrases, or codes) used to index the file. For example, if you use the thesaurus to look up "market research," you could find related terms, such as "consumer attitudes," "demographics," and "market research companies." These help tools vary greatly from database to database. Using these tools helps in the construction of accurate and cost-effective searches.

- Proximity selection, which allows searching of words or terms in specified relationships. With proximity operators, you can specify word order, words to be adjacent, near (within a selected number of words), or in the same section of the document (paragraph or title, for example).

- A wide variety of output formats, such as titles, bibliographic citations, mailing labels, or full text. In addition, you can frequently output custom-designed reports.

- Search feedback, such as a search history and the numbers of retrievals found in each search. This feedback allows the searcher to modify tactics and improve search results.

- A report of the size and price of predicted output so that sizable downloads do not overwhelm small-capacity computers or cost too much.

- Inexpensive or free browse formats such as KWIC (Key Word In Context), which provides highlighted search terms with text displayed on either side. This helps the searcher to select the best results, particularly in full-text databases.

- Set building (search refinement by steps, or sets), which is the ability to return to and modify a previous search statement.

Table 6-1 shows a brief comparison of commands provided in the DataStar and DIALOG systems. It shows the power, complexity, and system-to-system variations in command languages.

Table 6-1
Commands Vary from One Service to Another— Examples from DataStar and DIALOG

General Functions	DataStar	DIALOG
To search	..s (If not in search mode)	s or ss
Basic index	All paragraphs	Varies by database
Next to each other and exact order	ADJ	(w) or (#w)
In any order, near each other	WITH	(n) or (#n)
In same paragraph or (sub)field	SAME	(s)
Restricted to specific fields	PUBLISHER.TI.	publisher/ti
File change	..CHANGE INVE (Databases have acronyms)	begin 545 (Databases have numbers)
Truncation	HARVEST$	s harvest?
View index (thesaurus)	..ROOT (Shows terms with exact stem) 1: .. ROOT MILLER.AU.	expand (Shows surrounding terms expand au=miller

(continued)

Table 6-1
(continued)

General Functions	DataStar	Dialog
Display sets	.. D 1–5	ds 1–5
Display documents	P 1 All 1–5	type s1/5/1–5
Pause to think	..PARK	pause
Disconnect	..O	logoff

One important task is finding the appropriate database or databases to search. Choosing the appropriate major service is the first step: pick one whose specialty matches your interest. Either DIALOG or LEXIS-NEXIS are good choices for the generalist, the business searcher, or the market researcher. Become expert in that major service, and know the others well enough so you can search when needed for special information.

Most of the database services have tools to help you find the best databases to search. They have catalogs with descriptions of all the databases—both in printed format and as online help files. DIALOG, for example, has "Bluesheets," which provides detailed descriptions of each database on DIALOG.

Another common tool is a method for searching many files at once to find out which files have information on your search terms. On DIALOG, this tool is called DIALINDEX; similar tools are available on other systems. In a typical DIALINDEX search, you specify a group of files, such as ALLBUSINESS (a group of more than 200 business-related files). You then specify your search statement, such as "(market OR markets) AND (research OR researches) AND (cost OR costs)." The results will tell you how many documents in each database meet your criteria so you may select the best database or databases. You can sort the output by the number of documents found.

Figure 6-1 shows the use of DIALOG DIALINDEX for that search. I selected (sf = select files) the grouping of files ALL-

DIALINDEX(R)

(c) 1995 Knight-Ridder Info

?sf allbusiness

You have 247 files in your file list.

?s market?(s)research?(s)cost?

Items	File
6953	15: ABI/INFORM(R)_1971-1995/Mar W4
9876	16: PTS Promt(TM)_1972-1995/Apr 05
1187	17: PTS Annual Reports Abstr.(R)_1991/May
16	18: PTS F&S INDEX(R)_1980-1995/MarW4
95	22: Employee Benefits_1986-1995/Apr

|
|

| 961 | 772: Textline Global News_1990-1992 |
| 2987 | 799: Textline Curr.Glob.News_1993-1995/Apr 05 |

183 files have one or more items; file list includes 247 files.

?rank files

Items	File
78975	545: Investext(R)_1982-1995/Apr 03
23336	541: SEC Online(TM) Annual Repts_1995/Mar W4
17749	542: SEC Online(TM) 10-K Reports_1995/Mar W4
10396	543: SEC Online(TM) 10-Q Reports_1995/Mar W4
9876	16: PTS Promt(TM)_1972-1995/Apr 05

BUSINESS, which includes 246 business-related files. The output lists results by number of items that match the search statement in each file. In this case, 183 files had at least one item about the cost of marketing research. Then, using the rank files command (rf), I asked the service to sort the list by number of items found. As you can see, Investext (the file containing investment analysts' reports) had the most items.

This type of search can perform other useful functions. You can pretest, at low cost, various Boolean search statements. You can quickly identify the existence and location of specific types of information. In another example, I wanted to find references to reports from The Gartner Group (a research company) about computer cost. By using DIAL-INDEX and the search terms GARTNER AND REPORT? AND COMPUTER? AND COST?, I found that ninety files had information. Files having the most information were Trade & Industry Database, Computer Database, Magazine Database, ABI/INFORM, PROMT, and PTS Newsletter DB. The DIALINDEX search is a very valuable asset to the market researcher.

Two publications provide valuable help on finding full-text databases and newspaper information online. One is *Newspapers Online: A Guide to Searching Daily Newspapers Whose Articles Are Online in Full Text*, edited by Susanne Bjorner and published by BiblioData. The other is *Fulltext Sources Online*, edited by Ruth M. Orenstein and also published by BiblioData. An example page from *Fulltext Sources Online* is shown in Figure 6-2.

Search Tools for the Future

New technologies will make it easier to maximize the productivity of online searching. For example, one feature called weighted relevance enables the researcher to know which of

Market Latin America *(Continued)*

NewsNet: IT30	01/94 - Pres.
STN: NLDB	10/93 - Pres.
▲ STN: PROMT	10/93 - Pres.
Westlaw: DIALOG ON WEST (PTS-NEWS)	10/93 - Pres.
▲ Westlaw: DIALOG ON WEST (PTS-PROMT)	10/93 - Pres.
Westlaw: DOW JONES ON WESTLAW	10/93 - Pres.

Market Place (United Kingdom)

▲ DataTimes: FT PROFILE (FT MCCARTHY)	1986 - 1990
▲ FT Profile: FT MCCARTHY	1986 - 1990

Market Research Europe

▲ Data-Star: IDZZ: TRADE & INDUSTRY	01/90 - Pres.
▲ DataTimes: TRIN: TRADE & INDUSTRY ASAP	01/90 - Pres.
▲ Dialog: 648: TRADE & INDUSTRY ASAP	01/90 - Pres.
▲ Mead Nexis: NEWS (ASAPII)	01/90 - Pres.
▲ Westlaw: DIALOG ON WEST (TI-ASAP)	01/90 - Pres.

Market Trends

Mead Nexis: WORLD (DBMKT)	01/93 - Pres.

Marketing (United Kingdom)

▲ CDP: INFO	01/92 - Pres.
▲ Data-Star: IDZZ: TRADE & INDUSTRY	01/90 - Pres.
▲ Data-Star: INFO	01/92 - Pres.
Data-Star: TX88: TEXTLINE	05/83 - 12/88
Freq: Weekly; Lag: 5 day	
Data-Star: TXLN: TEXTLINE	01/91 - Pres.
Freq: Weekly; Lag: 5 day	
Data-Star: TXYY: TEXTLINE	01/89 - Pres.
Freq: Weekly; Lag: 5 day	
DataTimes: FT PROFILE	09/85 - Pres.
▲ DataTimes: TRIN: TRADE & INDUSTRY ASAP	01/90 - Pres.
▲ Dialog: 15: ABI/INFORM	01/92 - Pres.
▲ Dialog: 648: TRADE & INDUSTRY ASAP	01/90 - Pres.
Dialog: TXTLN (TEXTLINE ONESEARCH)	05/83 - Pres.
Freq: Weekly; Lag: 5 day	
▲ FT Profile: ABI	01/92 - Pres.
FT Profile: MKT	09/85 - Pres.
FT Profile: TLALL: TEXTLINE	05/83 - Pres.
Freq: Weekly; Lag: 5 day	
▲ Info Globe: ABI	01/92 - Pres.
▲ Mead Nexis: NEWS (ASAPII)	01/90 - Pres.
▲ Mead Nexis: NEWS (MRKTNG)	01/90 - Pres.
Mead Nexis: WORLD: TXTLNE	05/83 - Pres.
Freq: Weekly; Lag: 5 day	
▲ STN: ABI-INFORM	01/92 - Pres.
▲ Westlaw: DIALOG ON WEST (ABI-INFORM)	01/92 - Pres.
Westlaw: DIALOG ON WEST (INT-NEWS)	05/83 - Pres.
Freq: Weekly; Lag: 5 day	
▲ Westlaw: DIALOG ON WEST (TI-ASAP)	01/90 - Pres.

Marketing & Media Decisions

See "Mediaweek" which replaces this publication in 1991.

▲ Data-Star: IDZZ: TRADE & INDUSTRY	01/83 - 01/91
▲ DataTimes: TRIN: TRADE & INDUSTRY ASAP	01/90 - 01/91
▲ Dialog: 648: TRADE & INDUSTRY ASAP	01/83 - 01/91
▲ Mead Nexis: NEWS (ASAPII)	01/83 - 01/91
▲ Westlaw: DIALOG ON WEST (TI-ASAP)	01/83 - 01/91

Marketing Computers

This is an Adweek publication.

▲ Data-Star: CMPT: COMPUTER DB	06/94 - Pres.
▲ Data-Star: IDZZ: TRADE & INDUSTRY	01/89 - Pres.
Data-Star: PTSP: PROMT	06/90 - Pres.
DataTimes: PRMT	06/90 - Pres.
(Continued, next column)	

Marketing Computers *(Continued)*

▲ DataTimes: TRIN: TRADE & INDUSTRY ASAP	01/90 - Pres.
Dialog: 16: PROMT	06/90 - Pres.
▲ Dialog: 648: TRADE & INDUSTRY ASAP	01/89 - Pres.
▲ Dialog: 675: COMPUTER ASAP	06/94 - Pres.
▲ Dow Jones: //TEXT: BUSINESS LIB	01/91 - Pres.
FT Profile: PRP: PROMT	06/90 - Pres.
Genios: PROM	10/92 - Pres.
Mead Nexis: MARKET (PROMTP)	06/90 - Pres.
▲ Mead Nexis: NEWS (ASAPII)	01/89 - Pres.
STN: PROMT	06/90 - Pres.
Westlaw: DIALOG ON WEST (PTS-PROMT)	06/90 - Pres.
▲ Westlaw: DIALOG ON WEST (TI-ASAP)	01/89 - Pres.

Marketing Intelligence & Planning

▲ CDP: INFO	07/92 - Pres.
▲ Data-Star: INFO	07/92 - Pres.
▲ Dialog: 15: ABI/INFORM	07/92 - Pres.
▲ FT Profile: ABI	07/92 - Pres.
▲ Info Globe: ABI	07/92 - Pres.
▲ STN: ABI-INFORM	07/92 - Pres.
▲ Westlaw: DIALOG ON WEST (ABI-INFORM)	07/92 - Pres.

Marketing Management

▲ CDP: INFO	01/93 - Pres.
▲ Data-Star: INFO	01/93 - Pres.
▲ Dialog: 15: ABI/INFORM	01/93 - Pres.
▲ FT Profile: ABI	01/93 - Pres.
▲ Info Globe: ABI	01/93 - Pres.
Mead Nexis: NEWS (MKTMGT)	01/92 - Pres.
▲ STN: ABI-INFORM	01/93 - Pres.
▲ Westlaw: DIALOG ON WEST (ABI-INFORM)	01/93 - Pres.

Marketing News

▲ CDP: INFO	01/91 - Pres.
▲ Data-Star: IDZZ: TRADE & INDUSTRY	01/89 - Pres.
▲ Data-Star: INFO	01/91 - Pres.
▲ DataTimes: TRIN: TRADE & INDUSTRY ASAP	01/90 - Pres.
▲ Dialog: 15: ABI/INFORM	01/91 - Pres.
▲ Dialog: 648: TRADE & INDUSTRY ASAP	01/89 - Pres.
▲ FT Profile: ABI	01/91 - Pres.
▲ Info Globe: ABI	01/91 - Pres.
▲ Mead Nexis: NEWS (ASAPII)	01/89 - Pres.
Mead Nexis: NEWS (MKNEWS)	01/91 - Pres.
▲ STN: ABI-INFORM	01/91 - Pres.
▲ Westlaw: DIALOG ON WEST (ABI-INFORM)	01/91 - Pres.
▲ Westlaw: DIALOG ON WEST (TI-ASAP)	01/89 - Pres.

Marketing Research

▲ CDP: INFO	01/92 - Pres.
▲ Data-Star: INFO	01/92 - Pres.
▲ Dialog: 15: ABI/INFORM	01/92 - Pres.
▲ FT Profile: ABI	01/92 - Pres.
▲ Info Globe: ABI	01/92 - Pres.
Mead Nexis: NEWS (MKTRES)	01/91 - Pres.
▲ STN: ABI-INFORM	01/92 - Pres.
▲ Westlaw: DIALOG ON WEST (ABI-INFORM)	01/92 - Pres.

Marketing Research Review

Data-Star: PTBN: PTS NEWSLETTER	10/91 - Pres.
▲ Data-Star: PTSP: PROMT	10/91 - Pres.
DataTimes: PRED: PTS NEWSLETTER	12/91 - Pres.
▲ DataTimes: PRMT	10/91 - Pres.
▲ Dialog: 16: PROMT	10/91 - Pres.
Dialog: 636: PTS NEWSLETTER	10/91 - Pres.
Dow Jones: //TEXT: PTS NEWSLETTER	12/91 - Pres.
▲ FT Profile: PRP: PROMT	10/91 - Pres.
▲ Genios: PROM	10/92 - Pres.
(Continued, next page)	

▲ - Selected articles from these periodicals are found online in fulltext. See page v at the front for clarification.

No Mark - All articles in these periodicals are found online in fulltext. See page v at the front for exceptions.

Page 209

Figure 6-2 A page from *Fulltext Sources Online* shows where marketing journals are available online in full text

a series of retrieved articles is most interesting, focusing subsequent research on the truly relevant articles. These search tools consider the locations (such as title or lead paragraph) and number of occurrences of your search terms in documents. Then they select and list the documents depending on the calculated relevance. (Individual vendors use different proprietary algorithms.)

Examples of these new tools are DIALOG's TARGET and LEXIS-NEXIS's FREESTYLE. These non-Boolean, weighted-relevance database search techniques retrieve a number of records (for example, fifty in TARGET), which are displayed in order of importance. According to a study reported by Carol Tenopir and Pamela Cahn in *Online* magazine, May 1994, testing of these systems showed very similar results compared to each other and to Boolean searching. However, I have found the results are different but overlap somewhat. These search tools are most effective when used (and are designed for use) with full-text databases.

One search methodology that has proven useful with such new tools is combining them with Boolean results. Successful results have been achieved by

- Just combining (using an OR) the separate results from a Boolean search and from a relevance search
- Using the relevance tool to reduce the size of a result set obtained with a Boolean search

Avoid using a relevance search tool by itself for a comprehensive search.

True natural-language interfaces are the dream capability for online searching. The hope is to give the computer search requests in conversational language. One would need only to ask "How much money was spent on secondary marketing research in 1995?" The computer would proceed from there by selecting where to search, generating search strategies, running the search, and then delivering the requested result. *Not yet!* The development of true natural-language interfaces (and the closely related intelligent agents) is moving very slowly.

While we still have to wait for the natural-language interface, other goals for future search software are quite achievable. Searchers need tools that combine ease of use, flexibility, a high percentage of retrieval of useful results, and efficiency (low cost). Other desirable improvements include

- External removal of duplicates to all files, particularly patent files
- Automatic thesaurus features, such as synonym expansion, alternate spellings (with British or American variants), and expansion of acronyms and abbreviations
- Weighted-term searching: let the user specify which terms are most important and specify their relative importance
- Controllable case sensitivity (available on LEXIS now)

Any experienced searcher has his or her own wish list of enhancements and changes.

Summary

Use the professional services because they have the best access, the highest-quality and most comprehensive data, and the best customer support. They are the most cost-effective data sources for information. My advice: Pick one professional service and invest the time and effort necessary to become a skillful searcher. The next two chapters will present details of many of the services and provide some example searches.

For Further Reading

1. *Newspapers Online: A Guide to Searching Daily Newspapers Whose Articles Are Online in Full Text*, third edition, edited by Susanne Bjorner (BiblioData, 1995). Call BiblioData at 800-247-6553 or write to P.O. Box 61, Needham Heights, MA 02194. This is an extremely valu-

able reference for the market researcher or information professional. It is a directory of almost 200 newspapers that are available online. The book tells you where to find the newspapers online and gives descriptions of the newspapers, including special features. It also offers search tips for each newspaper.

2. *Directory of Business and Financial Information Services,* ninth edition, by Charles J. Popovich and Rita M. Costello (Special Libraries Association, 1994). It contains over 1240 abstracted titles and works of 3720 business specialty publishers, including print, online, and CD-ROM formats.

3. *Fulltext Sources Online,* edited by Ruth M. Orenstein (BiblioData—see reference 1 for ordering information). A must-have reference. *Fulltext Sources Online* is published twice a year, in January and June. It lists where periodicals, newspapers, newsletters, newswires, and TV/radio transcripts are available online. It allows one to find these sources by name, location, or topic. I use it every day. It is also available online on DataStar.

4. "Black Holes in Full-Text Databases," by Ruth Orenstein, *Database,* October 1993. An interesting article that describes just what is full text. She also points out that the definition of *full text* is not constant as you change databases.

5. **Vendor publications.** All the database publishers and suppliers offer extensive documentation, much of it free. When you find a database or service you like, get their documentation.

While not free, published thesauruses are particularly valuable for the professional searcher. They support preplanning precise searches offline for the best and lowest-cost results. Three that I own and use are

Search Tools, the Guide to UNI Online, second edition, (UMI, 1993). This comprehensive guide to the UMI databases (ABI/INFORM, Business Dateline, Newspapers and Periodical Abstracts, and others) is published by UMI, 620 South Third Street, Louisville KY, 40202 (502-538-4111).

Standard Industrial Classification Manual (SIC 2+2) (Dunn & Bradstreet Information Resources, 1989). This book is published by Dunn & Bradstreet Information Resources (800-234-3867). It provides both the United States government SIC codes and the Dunn & Bradstreet extensions.

Information Access Company Online User's Manual (Information Access Company, 1994). This is a complete guide to the large family of Information Access Company databases, including PROMPT, Trade and Industry Magazine Database, Computer Database, Global*base,* and many others. It is published by Information Access Company, Corporate Division, 362 Lakeside Drive, Foster City, CA 94404 (800-321-6388).

6. **Magazines.** There are many magazines that cover the world of professional databases. Three of the ones I always read are
   - *Searcher*, published ten times a year by Learned Information, Inc. (609-654-6266). An opinionated magazine that offers industry news and information.
   - *Database* and *Online*, each published six times a year by Online, Inc. (203-761-1466). These two magazines, published in alternate months, provide professional views of the industry and very practical search tips and methodologies.

7. **Newsletters.** Newsletters on the information industry show up in my mailbox every week—but I subscribe to only two of them. Those are *Information Broker*, published six times a year by Burwell Enterprises, Inc. (713-537-9051), and *The Information Advisor*, published monthly by FIND/SVP (212-645-4500). Both newsletters are published by and written by information professionals. I find something useful in every issue.

7 | *The Professional Services—Descriptions*

This chapter describes the major professional databases, particularly those with significant business information. This chapter will help you decide which services to purchase and learn.

Knight-Ridder DIALOG Information Services

The DIALOG service, from Knight-Ridder Information, Inc., is the world's largest online information research service. Since its beginning in 1972, DIALOG has been a major provider to librarians and professional researchers. DIALOG is very strong in business, science, technology, and intellectual property.

DIALOG contains information from documents, magazines, and journals covering scientific, technical, medical, business, trade, and academic issues. In addition, more than 100 full-text newspapers worldwide are available. With more than 450 databases covering a broad range of disciplines, it could satisfy the majority of the secondary marketing researcher's needs. Several search options are available:

- DIALOG menus are for those new to online searching or for searching databases that you use infrequently. Custom menu interfaces for specific applications are available. One new interface, KR ScienceBase, is planned for the use of scientific professionals and will be available on the World Wide Web.

- The DIALOG command language offers the fastest and most precise way to search for information.
- DIALOG's relevance ranking tool, TARGET, provides easy searching for the most-meaningful full-text articles.

Knight-Ridder Information, Inc., provides a broad range of support to the DIALOG searcher. A toll-free customer assistance hotline can be reached within the United States and Canada Monday through Friday, 8:00 A.M. to 8:00 P.M. eastern standard time (800-334-2564). Voicemail coverage is provided at night and on weekends.

Training is available for all user levels. Introductory full-day and half-day seminars acquaint new users with DIALOG. Self-instructional training tools are also available, including online training files, which allow inexpensive practice. Specialized training programs for information professionals cover business, chemistry, patents, government, and legal research.

Comprehensive support literature is available. In addition, there are several online databases and extensive online help messages to assist the user at any point in the search process. Support literature includes

- Individual Reference Guides for most databases
- An introductory guide to the DIALOG search system, entitled *Getting Started on DIALOG: A Guide to Searching*
- *Super Searching*, a guide to precision search techniques

A wide variety of documentation is available through an automated fax delivery service. Call 800-496-4470 or 415-496-4470 to order documents. Visit DIALOG on the Internet at http://www.dialog.com for additional easily available information.

DIALOG Databases

The *DIALOG Database Catalogue* is the best way to start work with the databases on the DIALOG system. This catalog, published annually by DIALOG, describes the key features of each available database. The catalog includes the following important sections:

- **Subject Guide.** A listing of databases by subject helps the researcher find the best database or databases. Subject groups include

  —Business and Industry

  —Business Statistics

  —International Directories and Company Financials

  —Product Information

  —U.S. Directories and Company Financials

  —Law and Government

  —Multidisciplinary—Books, General Information, and Reference

  —News—Newspaper Indexes, U.S. Newspapers Full Text, and Worldwide News

  —Patents, Trademarks, and Copyrights

  —Science—Agriculture and Nutrition, Chemistry, Computer Technology, Energy and Environment, Medicine and Biosciences, Pharmaceuticals, and Technology and Engineering

  —Social Sciences and Humanities

- **Database Descriptions.** An alphabetical listing of short summaries for each database. Each database is individually priced; search costs depend on the amount of connection time.

- **DIALINDEX/OneSearch Categories.** These predefined groups of files help in finding the right database for the information you need. Databases are grouped by subject coverage.

Many of the important business-related databases available on DIALOG are listed here:

- ABI/INFORM
- Accounting and Tax Database
- Aerospace/Defense Markets and Technology
- American Banker Full Text
- BCC Market Research
- BioCommerce Abstracts and Directory
- Business Dateline
- Corporate Affiliations
- D&B Market Identifiers
- Datamonitor Market Research
- Derwent World Patents Index
- DMS/FI Market Intelligence Reports
- Economic Literature Index
- Euromonitor Market Research
- Federal Acquisition Regulations (FARS)
- Freedonia Market Research
- Harvard Business Review
- Industry Trends and Analysis
- Investext
- McGraw-Hill Publications Online
- Marketing and Advertising Reference Service
- Newspaper and Periodical Abstracts
- PROMT
- SEC Online
- Standard & Poor's Register—Biographical
- Trade and Industry Database
- Tradeline and Tradeline International
- TRADEMARKSCAN

DIALOG
Special Features

The DIALOG service has many special features to improve service, simplify use, and meet special user requirements. Many of these special features are briefly described next.

DIALOG Business Connection

A menu-based service, DIALOG Business Connection (DBC) provides easy answers to a variety of business questions. It is organized as seven separate applications:

- Worldwide Corporate Intelligence
- Financial Screening
- Products and Markets
- Worldwide Sales Prospecting
- Travel Planning
- DIALOG Business News
- DIALOG Alert Service

DIALOG Alert Service

DIALOG Alert is a current-awareness service that provides continuous, up-to-date information on specified topics. (Current-awareness services are also called SDIs—Selective Dissemination of Information.) Create Alert profiles to monitor worldwide news about your company and its competitors, to track technological advances, to identify new business opportunities, and to keep track of regulations and legislation. Updates are sent automatically by first-class mail, fax, or electronic mail.

Dialmail

Dialmail is an electronic mail service that allows you to communicate with Knight-Ridder staff, information providers, and other DIALOG users. Dialmail also provides rapid delivery of printouts via your electronic mailbox. This electronic delivery feature enables you to receive search results within two hours.

DIALORDER

An online document-ordering service, DIALORDER allows you to request copies of original publications from a wide variety of document suppliers. This is an area where many improvements are occurring, such as low-cost delivery via the Internet.

DIALOG SourceOne

SourceOne is a worldwide document-delivery service that provides high-quality copies of original patent documents, journal articles, proceedings, standards, and other types of documents. This service is expanding, with access to many more sources and better delivery options that include full image delivery via the Internet.

DIALINDEX

DIALINDEX is a database selection tool that reviews many databases at a time to find the files that have the most information on your specific topic. The output is the number of results per database that match the search statement.

OneSearch

OneSearch allows the simultaneous searching of multiple databases. For example, you may search all the patent databases at once.

DialogLink

Communications software for personal computers running DOS, Windows, or the Macintosh operating system allows easy access to DIALOG and DataStar (another online service from Knight-Ridder). Network versions are also available. DialogLink features

- Automatic logon
- Search creation prior to going online
- Manipulating and printing captured or downloaded information
- Saving records to disk
- Cost accounting
- Image viewing
- Unlimited scrolling to review records

Images currently available for viewing include trademarks from U.S. FEDERAL TRADEMARKSCAN, chemical structures from Chapman and Hall Chemical Database, and patent drawings from Derwent World Patents Index. DialogLink also can be used as a convenient communications program for many other online services.

DIALOG Menus

The menu system provides a user-friendly alternative to command searching. It is ideal for online searchers who are not familiar with the commands. The menus provide easy access to the DIALOG databases.

DIALOG ERA

DIALOG ERA is a unique Electronic Redistribution and Archive procedure that makes paying copyright fees for multiple copies easy. It allows you legally to send copies of search results to coworkers or to store them in an in-house database.

DIALOG DIRECT

DIALOG DIRECT is a fully automated information service that delivers prepublication pharmaceutical, health care, and agrochemical news via the Internet.

REPORT

The REPORT command allows selection of individual data elements—such as company name, address, and annual sales. Then it organizes those elements into tables. It makes telemarketing lists, financial data comparisons, and other tables that can be exported to spreadsheet programs for further analysis and manipulation.

Knight-Ridder DataStar

The DataStar Information Retrieval Service has been serving its users since 1981. It is Europe's leading online service, providing more than 400 databases covering a broad range of disciplines. It has powerful search tools and a complete online help system. DataStar is global partner to the DIALOG system. Although some files are on both systems, many items on DataStar are not available on DIALOG. For information and a DataStar database catalog, contact the DIALOG/Data-Star Help Desk at 800-221-7754 (in the United States). Information is also available on the Internet at http://www.rs.ch.

DataStar provides training seminars for beginners and advanced users. Free training databases are available online. Documentation includes a system reference manual, the *DataStar Guide,* which describes all the commands and tools available. Reference guides to all of the databases are also available.

DataStar offers some important service databases to help the searcher. The CROS database is an index to all the available databases; a simple search request returns a list of databases that include information on your topic. The NEWS database provides the latest information about DataStar. The BASE database describes all the available databases.

DataStar excels in comprehensive global coverage of automotive industry data, detailed import/export trade statistics, and specialized pharmaceutical, biomedical, and health care information. It also has a unique collection of European information, newspapers, and newswires. You'll have easy access to detailed import/export statistics in TRADSTAT Plus, an award-winning database offering full statistics for twenty-four countries around the world. The following is a list of some of the most important business files available on DataStar but not on DIALOG:

- Automotive Information and News
- BDI German Industry
- Infotrade: Belgian Company Financial Data
- International Business Opportunities Service
- Infocheck British Company Financial Datasheets
- Computer Industry Software, Services, and Products
- Credit Suisse: Information on the Swiss Economy
- Corporate Technology: U.S. high-tech companies
- Dun & Bradstreet Eastern Europe Marketing File
- Pharma Marketing Service (PMS)
- ABC EUROPE: European Export Industry
- Country Report Service
- International Market Research Information
- Market Structure and Trends in Italy
- MarketLine International Reports
- Management and Marketing Abstracts
- Quest Economics Database
- Who Makes Machinery and Plant
- Who Owns Whom

LEXIS-NEXIS

LEXIS-NEXIS is an extremely valuable full-text online service offering business, news, and legal information. The company is a division of Reed Elsevier PLC, one of the world's leading publishing and information companies. Reed Elsevier has headquarters in London; the LEXIS-NEXIS division is based in Dayton, Ohio.

One of the pioneers in the online information industry, the LEXIS service began operation in 1973 to help legal professionals research the law more efficiently. Today, information specialists, marketers, accountants, financial analysts, journalists, and lawyers perform an estimated 200,000 searches a day on the LEXIS service and its companion, the NEXIS news and information service. (NEXIS began in 1979.) There are more than 5000 databases in LEXIS-NEXIS. More than 2.5 million documents are added each week.

LEXIS-NEXIS organizes data sources into groups called libraries. In the most common billing method, users are charged a fixed price per search: the charge varies depending on the library chosen. Three different options of searching for information are provided: FREESTYLE, Boolean, and Easy Search:

- The FREESTYLE feature is a relevance search tool that uses plain English input for searching both legal and non-legal materials.

- The Boolean search option provides precision researching for experienced users.

- The Easy Search feature displays online menus and screen prompts to assist novice users in formulating precise search requests and then selects the correct parts of the database to search.

The LEXIS-NEXIS services publish many documents to help searchers. *The Directory of Online Services* (with a new edition in 1995) lists all the basic information needed to use the services, including all the current databases in the 166 libraries. Customer service provides regular newsletters and faxes describing additions and changes to the services. Useful search tips are published in documents such as the recently released LEXIS-NEXIS *Competitive Intelligence Search Tips.*

Online, LEXIS-NEXIS provides many helpful guides, grouped files, and libraries to aid searchers. Extensive free training is available over the telephone and at LEXIS-NEXIS offices. Online practice libraries are also available.

LEXIS-NEXIS has well-trained and very helpful customer service representatives available twenty-four hours a day, seven days a week (except for a short period early Sunday morning). They can help with any questions about signing on and using the services. They can also help with the proper selection of databases and search strategies. Customer Service numbers are

- LEXIS (U.S. only): 800-543-6862
- NEXIS (U.S. only): 800-346-9759

LEXIS-NEXIS can also be reached on the Internet at http://www.lexis-nexis.com.

LEXIS-NEXIS Databases

NEXIS

NEXIS is a comprehensive full-text news and business information service. The NEWS library of current and archived news and information contains more than 2400 full-text sources. The NEXIS service is the exclusive online archival source (at least until the end of 1995) for the *New York Times* in the legal, business, and other professional markets. NEXIS also carries other major news publications, including the *Washington Post, Los Angeles Times, Business Week, Fortune,* and the *Economist.* The service includes both national network and regional television broadcast transcripts, in addition to carrying Cable News Network and National Public Radio news and features.

Major news services of the unified Russian republics, Japan, China, United States, Britain, France, Mexico, and Germany are vital sources of international business information and news. In addition, the NEXIS service contains more than 2000 sources of abstracts, including the *Wall Street Journal.*

Many user-friendly features are provided. The NEWS library groups relate news items into types, such as international, non-English-language, and full-text general news, financial materials, and directories. The Top News (TOPNWS) library contains same-day news from selected key sources from around the world, including newswires—the Associated Press, Reuters, Agence-France Press, and Xinhua—and major metropolitan newspapers.

Users also can select libraries by topic. The NEXIS Market library, for instance, focuses on marketing and industry news by specific industry. Topics libraries include banks, business and finance, computers and communications, energy, entertainment, and environment. NEXIS service "hot files" are placed online within twenty-four hours in some cases when rapid-fire developments in domestic or foreign affairs create extraordinary interest among users. These special files combine information from many sources in many different libraries.

> EDGAR (Electronic Data Gathering, Analysis, and Retrieval system) was started in 1993 by the SEC to update the gathering of corporate information by changing from paper to electronic data submittal. By the planned 1996 completion, all public companies (more than 14,000) will be filing electronically.

One very important source on NEXIS is EDGAR Plus, offered through Disclosure, Inc. Tracking public companies can be very important for the market researcher. EDGAR Plus allows enhanced access to SEC filings and a series of SEC products developed from EDGAR data.

LEXIS

The LEXIS service is a major source of legal information. It has forty-five specialized libraries, covering all major fields of practice, including tax, securities, banking, environment, energy, and international. LEXIS contains

- Archives of federal and state case law
- Continuously updated statutes of all fifty states
- State and federal regulations
- Public records from many U.S. states

The convenient group files combine legal information from all jurisdictions and, in some cases, add sources of relevant business, financial, or general news.

The Hot Topics library contains summaries of the latest legal and regulatory developments within about forty practice areas. The Begin Research library contains American Law Institute Restatements of the Law, American Law reports, annotated case citations, and selected state jurisprudence. It is a great place to start looking at secondary legal research materials.

The LEXIS service also contains international information, with libraries of English, French, and Canadian law. Legal materials from Australia, New Zealand, Ireland, and Scotland are also available.

LEXIS has a full complement of research tools, including an online Guide, providing detailed descriptions of all NEXIS and selected LEXIS libraries. Other important tools are Shepard's citation service, Auto-Cite citation service, and the FOCUS feature, which highlights keywords in a search result.

FOCUS can be particularly useful. (It's also free.) The FOCUS feature enables you to narrow your search results set to a subset matching additional search terms. You can use it at any search level and as often as you like. (You cannot use the FOCUS feature on FOCUS results.) You can use the FOCUS feature after you have run a search, either before or after reviewing the results. Issue the FOCUS command (type .fo and press ENTER) and just follow the screen instructions. FOCUS acts as an AND modification because it searches within search results already found.

LEXIS-NEXIS Special Features

Many valuable services come with a LEXIS-NEXIS subscription. For one, LEXIS-NEXIS provides excellent and easy-to-use search software. The current Windows version has buttons for many common commands and an extensive help system. Subscribers receive this valuable LEXIS-NEXIS research software in formats compatible with Macintosh, DOS, and Windows.

Market Quick & Easy

Market Quick & Easy is a new front-end software package. Released in the spring of 1995, it provides easy access to the business information in LEXIS-NEXIS. Menus are custom designed for specific applications—in this case, marketing research.

LEXIS Financial Information Service

The LEXIS Financial Information Service provides business and financial news, SEC filings, brokerage house research reports, private company market share information, and real-time and historical stock quotes from all North American exchanges.

Country Information Service

LEXIS Country Information Service contains international news and analysis reports by country, region, and topic. It also offers the ALERT file, which carries news updated every three hours. International files can be searched all at once, individually, or by the following regions: Asia/Pacific Rim, Middle East and Africa, North and South America, and Europe. The Associated Press Political Service contains information on elections, political issues, polls, and candidates.

National Automated Accounting Research System

The National Automated Accounting Research System (NAARS) provides accounting materials, including annual reports of public corporations and government entities, and reports of the American Institute of Certified Public Accountants.

MEDIS Service

The MEDIS Service offers full-text medical information from the publications of the American Society of Hospital Pharmacists, the National Cancer Institute, and FDC Reports, Inc. Bibliographic research may be done in the Medline database produced by the National Library of Medicine, which indexes more than 3600 medical journals.

LEXPAT Service

The LEXPAT Service contains the full text of patent information for more than 1.5 million U.S. patents issued since 1975. About 75,000 new patents are added each year, usually within four days of issue. Trademark information is also available.

ECLIPSE

The ECLIPSE (Electronic Clipping Service) feature automatically reports new materials that correspond to a saved search request. The reports can be issued daily, every business day, weekly, or monthly.

LEXDOC

The LEXDOC feature allows LEXIS-NEXIS subscribers to order copies of public records documents retrieved from any jurisdiction—state or local—in the country. Public records filed in Canada and the Virgin Islands are also available. Orders are handled by LEXIS Document Services.

LEXIS Public Records Online Service

The LEXIS Public Records Online Service is a powerful litigation research tool that provides online access to information from selected states about real and personal property assets, Uniform Commercial Code (UCC) liens, secretary of state corporation filings, verdicts, settlements, and court indices. LEXIS Document Services provides prompt nationwide access to searching and filing of hard-copy UCC, corporate, tax lien, and judgment documents. With a toll-free telephone call, filings and search requests are fulfilled at both state and local levels in all fifty states plus the District of Columbia.

DataTimes

DataTimes is a leading regional, international, and business news bank. The DataTimes service covers more than 5000 full-text and numeric sources, including newswires, regional and national newspapers, and international sources. DataTimes introduced major changes to its service in the spring of 1995 with a new graphics interface and pricing structure.

EyeQ is the new Windows-based graphical user interface. (A DOS interface is also available, as a separate program.) EyeQ provides many new features, including a search help system, called Mentor, that narrows search results by suggesting appropriate terms (such as company names and topics) specific to immediate search contexts. Database selection is made from prearranged topic groups. Searchers can choose specific sources, if desired. The EyeQ system provides industry codes, suggested search terms, and lists of industries to guide the searcher. The new system primarily uses a natural-language interface with relevance ranking. Boolean search commands are also available at any time.

The new single pricing structure covers all text sources, with a flat monthly fee for searching and per-article charges for downloading. There are no connect-time charges or charges for reviewing headlines. Some special outputs, such as the Executive Reports, have higher prices. You are informed of the price prior to incurring the charge.

The DataTimes network contains more than 5000 sources from the United States and around the world, including the following:

- Newspapers from forty-eight states, Washington, D.C., and many countries
- National magazines and real-time newswires
- Trade sources and newsletters that serve 120 industries
- Broadcast transcripts for the top TV news programs—from CBS, NBC, CNBC, CNN, and PBS—as well as National Public Radio
- Financial data, quotes, and commentary
- Newsletters
- Executive Reports on 30,000 U.S. and international companies

When you log on to EyeQ, you are presented with six options, plus a bulletin board that notifies you of messages or announcements. The six options are

- **Search.** Searches more than 5000 local, regional, national, and international sources.

- **Business Analyst.** Combines the best products from American Business Information, Disclosure, Inc., Investext, PC Quote, Standard & Poor's, TRW Business Credit Summary, Worldscope, Tradeline, and others.

- **Private Eye.** Sifts through thousands of sources to find information you specify on an ongoing and automatic basis. This is the alert service.

- **Today's News.** Retrieves up-to-date business news from around the world via regional newspapers and national wire services.

- **Executive Reports.** Provides 30,000 reports on public and private U.S. and international companies, as well as 178 industries, along with prices for each report.

- **Customer Service.** Displays your Billing History or Customer Information. Messages are also sent to and received from Customer Service.

Business Analyst is a particularly useful tool for the marketing researcher. It can provide detailed information for business decisions. For example, it can deliver financial and stock market information on thousands of companies and industries. Business Analyst is divided into two main functions:

- **Quick Reports.** Provides predefined reports for a particular company. You enter the company name and then choose from the following available reports: Stock, Profile, Annual, Quarterly, or Analyst.

- **Analysis Tools.** Creates a custom report about a selected company. Several report categories are available: Company Reports, Industry Reports, Comparisons, Market Master, Business Credit, Business Directory+, and Portfolio Manager.

On the new system, searchers can receive customized "Executive Reports." These are company profiles with current data covering 20,000 publicly traded U.S. and international companies, as well as some 7000 privately held U.S. companies. Data includes company and industry descriptions, top executives, recent news headlines, financial results, and performance trends. The reports are available by electronic mail, fax, print, or online. Another type of report, Industry Scorecards, provides comprehensive briefings on 178 industries—leading industry players, relative market share, industry trends, rankings by size, growth, and so on.

DataTimes can be reached at 800-642-2525.

Profound

Profound is a new Windows-based online service offered by Profound, Inc. Ltd., as agent for M.A.I.D PLC., a corporate supplier of market research. Profound supplies news headlines, company financial reports, market reports, broker reports, and country research reports. (Profound also offers a networked corporate version.) The structure and pricing of the package are very similar to the new DataTimes EyeQ product. A unique feature is its use of Adobe Acrobat software to provide full-color graphical output identical to the original reports. For more information on Profound, call 800-851-1229 or 212-750-6900.

The Profound software interface consists of six icons that provide access to the various information groups. To proceed, you select an icon:

- **Briefings.** Offers a quick overview on markets, companies, and economies in graphic format.
- **Custom Alert.** Provides automatic alerts on specific topics of interest.

- **NewsNow.** Reports current news, updated hourly from Associated Press, Extel, AFX, and other newswires.
- **Quotes.** Presents current and historical prices for stocks, futures, metals, and foreign currencies.
- **AutoSearch.** Utilizes a natural-language search interface.
- **Utilities.** Offers account and billing information.

Selecting the Briefings icon accesses four additional icons:

- **Market Briefings.** Market surveys on more than 300 consumer, retail, and industrial markets, covering the United States, Japan, Germany, France, and the United Kingdom.
- **Country Briefings.** Surveys of the economies of more than 100 major countries.
- **S&P Stock Reports.** Five-page reports on more than 4600 U.S. public companies, from Standard & Poor's.
- **Company Briefings.** Reports on more than 20,000 public companies worldwide, from Disclosure/Worldscope.

Profound offers two search methods (screens) for retrieving information from the databases: AutoSearch is a point-and-click menu system that automatically accesses the InfoSort Navigator (a built-in thesaurus) to help you select the appropriate search terms. It guides you through data retrieval one step at a time. WorldSearch is a more powerful tool; it allows you to use Boolean logic and provides more control over the search. InfoSort Navigator may be accessed for help.

The following six databases are accessed through World-Search:

- **Researchline** includes more than 40,000 market research reports from the world's leading publishers, such as Frost and Sullivan, FIND/SVP, The Freedonia Group, BCC, Packaged Facts, Theta Corporation, Pyramid Research, Insight Research, and USA Monitor.
- **Newsline** accesses more than 4700 newspapers, magazines, and trade journals from 190 countries, translated from seventeen languages. Publishers include Reuters, Information Access Company, and UMI.

- **Wireline** is real-time news from Associated Press, AFX, Extel, Knight-Ridder, and others.
- **Companyline** has full financial reports from leading publishers on millions of companies worldwide. Publishers include Dun & Bradstreet, Disclosure, Extel, and Hemmington Scott.
- **Brokerline** provides more than 40,000 analysts' reports from top international brokerage houses.
- **Countryline** offers country reports, economic forecasts, and analyses on 180 countries worldwide from EIU and other publishers.

NewsNet

NewsNet is the primary source for industry-specific business newsletters. NewsNet publishes online about 800 newsletters, ranging from *Access Reports/Freedom of Information* to *Worldwide Videotext Update*. NewsNet also accesses newswires from UPI, AP, Knight-Ridder, and others. Gateway service is provided to American Business Information, Dun & Bradstreet, and TRW Business Profiles.

NewsNet has a long list of titles applicable to marketing research in many categories. Some of the categories and titles include

- Advertising and marketing
  - *American Marketplace*
  - *Product Alert*
- Electronics and computers
  - *The Business Computer*
  - *CD-ROM Databases*
  - *Electronic Business Forecast*
- General business
- Management

- Publishing and broadcasting
  —*New Media Markets*
  —*Online Newsletter*
  —*Ratings Advertising Programming*
- Telecommunications

NewsNet offers a complete range of customer services, including a new Windows interface called BATON. Complete documentation and training are part of the package. NewsFlash is the easy-to-use electronic-clipping or current-awareness feature. Contact NewsNet at 800-952-0122.

I/PLUS Direct

I/PLUS Direct is the online service of the Investext Group of Thompson Financial Services. It provides direct access to a wide range of company and industry overviews, investment reports, and market research information. I/PLUS Direct offers

- **Investext analyst research reports.** More than 700,000 reports, dating from 1982.
- **Fortune Private Company Profiles.** Information on more than 1500 private U.S. companies in an easy-to-use format.
- **Fortune Industry Scorecards.** Overviews on 178 industries.
- **Pipeline.** Rapid access to more than 80,000 of the very latest analyst research reports and company profiles.
- **MarkIntel.** Expert industry and market intelligence from 35,000 full-text market research reports from twenty-two sources. Eight of these sources are exclusive to MarkIntel.
- **SEC Online, American Banker Online, and Bond Buyer Online.**

I/PLUS Direct is an easy-to-use, fully menu-driven system with complete documentation available. You can search by company name, ticker symbol, industry, geographic region, business subject, type of project, and more. Output comes as individual report pages or as the whole report. Contact I/PLUS Direct at 800-662-7878 for more details.

Dow Jones

Dow Jones News/Retrieval (DJNR) is the full-text online service of Dow Jones and Company—the publisher of the *Wall Street Journal*. DJNR is a very important service for business—it has exclusive full-text access to the *Wall Street Journal* and other Dow Jones publications. DJNR offers access to the following:

- Business and World Newswires, such as the new Emerging Market Report.
- Dow Jones Text Library of more than 1800 publications, including the *Financial Times* and the *Wall Street Journal*.
- Company and Industry Information—business and financial data on about 10 million U.S. and international companies in eighty databases.
- Quotes, Market Data, and Analysis (including historical data).
- Nikkei Telecom, which is now available via a new gateway. Nikkei Telecom is the most extensive English-language source on Japan and the Far East. Produced by the publisher of the *Nihon Keizai Shimbun*, Nikkei Telecom provides access to eleven news services, more than 1 million articles, corporate profiles of companies, and annual stock data dating back to 1964.
- A variety of general services, including

  —BOOKS: Magill Book Reviews

  —ENCYC: Academic American Encyclopedia

  —MOVIES: Cineman Movie Reviews

  —OAG: Official Airline Guides

—WTHR: Dow Jones Weather Report

—CAREER: National Business Employment Weekly

Support publications include the Reference Guide, a Text Library Reference Guide, and a Publications Directory. The Reference Guide includes descriptions of all DJNR services, plus tips and tactics for using them—such as hints on using full-text sources and a quick guide to using search codes. The Text Library Reference Guide provides searching tips for anyone interested in searching the DJNR library.

The Publications Directory lists all of the publications available in DJNR's vast Text Library, including each publication's start date, source code, publication frequency, and when the publication is available online. The information is available for the more than 1800 publications in the library. This directory also includes geographic, industry, and other codes you can use in your searches.

Very easy to use new software was released in April 1995. This software provides point-and-click access to all of the features of Dow Jones News/Retrieval. Searching can be done by command language or by menus.

Extensive online help is available, including a Code Directory, pricing information, updates, and network access numbers. DJNR also provides an alert service called Dow Jones Custom-Clips. Additional help and information is available from customer service (609-452-1511). Customer service representatives are available Monday through Friday from 8 A.M. to midnight, and Saturday from 9 A.M. to 6 P.M. (Eastern Time).

Other Services

WESTLAW

WESTLAW is the online legal research service provided by West Publishing, a preeminent legal publisher. On WESTLAW, you can access case law, federal codes, federal rules and regulations, state statutes, specialized databases (such as bankruptcy or tax), and much more. Although WESTLAW is not focused on business, both DIALOG and Dow Jones are accessible through WESTLAW, allowing complete access to business information. WESTLAW has an award-winning natural-language interface called WIN (for WESTLAW Is Natural) and extensive user support. Westmate software is available for Windows and DOS.

STN

STN International is an online service provided in North America by Chemical Abstracts Service. STN is an outstanding scientific database with exceptional chemical coverage. Although not primarily a business database, it is important to researchers whose market is scientific. STN provides access to two important English-language Japanese technology databases—JCIST-E and JGRIP. Call STN at 800-753-4227 or 800-848-6533.

STN (the Scientific and Technical Information Network) provides direct access to over 190 scientific, technical, business, and patent databases to users worldwide. STN is operated jointly by CAS in North America, by the Japan Information Center of Science and Technology (JICST) in Asia, and by FIZ-Karlsruhe in Germany for users in Europe.

STN is on the Internet on the CAS home page at http://info.cas.org. One very useful item on the Web site is a tutorial on using STN. This tutorial includes Online Searching Basics, Search Strategy, Text Searching, Author Name Searching, Refining Searches, Substance Searching, Online Searching Costs, and Practice Problems. It is suitable for independent study.

CAS provides a number of customer support services that can help you with everything from getting started with online searching on STN to answering specific questions concerning search strategies and database content. STN

Workshops, Technical Sessions, and User Meetings provide personalized, hands-on training to help customers make the most effective use of their online searching time.

Questel-Orbit

Questel-Orbit is an international online information company whose emphasis is on patent, trademark, scientific, chemical, business, and news information. The service provides current awareness, online document ordering, online index to databases (PowerIndex), multifile searching (Power-Search and Plus 2), and online patent drawings. Databases are available for

- Business
- Chemical information
- Energy and earth sciences
- Engineering
- Health, safety, and the environment
- Humanities and social sciences
- Materials science
- Medicine
- News
- Patents
- Science and technology
- Trademarks

Questel-Orbit can be contacted at 800-955-0906.

Summary

The database services described in this chapter (except for WESTLAW and Questel-Orbit) are services I currently use for business and marketing research. Though it is not required that you have access to all of the listed sources, each service has one or more unique and valuable databases (such as the *Wall Street Journal* on Dow Jones). Therefore, a comprehensive search can require the use of several services.

The best way to use multiple services efficiently is to pick one service (I suggest DIALOG or LEXIS-NEXIS) and become very proficient. Then use menu systems or simplified commands to search the others when necessary. I currently use DIALOG as my primary resource. I use DataStar, LEXIS-NEXIS, DJNR, NewsNet, STN, and I/PLUS for special topics or specific resources like the *Wall Street Journal* on DJNR.

Significant changes are occurring in the professional information services industry. The new interfaces and pricing structures of DataTimes and Profound may have a major impact on the pricing structures of the largest providers such as DIALOG and LEXIS-NEXIS. The emphasis on end-user searching will change the market structure of the industry.

For Further Reading

No additional reading is recommended, except the sources provided by the online services. Here is a list of customer service phone numbers (and, where available, World Wide Web addresses):

- Knight-Ridder DIALOG: 800-334-2564; http://www.dialog.com
- Knight-Ridder DataStar: 800-221-7754; http://www.rs.ch
- LEXIS-NEXIS: 800-227-4908, 800-227-8379 (in Ohio); http://www.lexis-nexis.com
- DataTimes: 800-642-2525
- Profound, Inc.: 800-851-1229 or 212-750-6900
- NewsNet: 800-952-0122
- I/PLUS Direct: 800-662-7878
- Dow Jones News/Retrieval: 609-452-1511
- West Publishing: 800-241-0244
- STN: 800-753-4227
- Questel-Orbit: 800-955-0906

8 | *Using the Professional Services for Secondary Marketing Research*

This chapter demonstrates, with simple examples, the use of the professional databases for secondary marketing research.

> For comparison purposes, I will repeat one search, called the Test Case, using the Internet (in Chapter 11) and the consumer databases (in Chapter 14).

DIALOG—Creating a Corporate Profile

In the first example, I will use databases on DIALOG to generate a typical corporate profile, a powerful tool for organizing information about competitors. I arbitrarily picked CDP Technologies for our example. As discussed in Chapter 2, develop a simple corporate profile by taking the following steps.

Find Basic Company Information from Directories

I will use Dun's Market Identifiers from Dun & Bradstreet in this example. This file provides (and can be searched for) company name, address, phone numbers, type of business, organization history, sales, and executives. Other useful directory databases include Disclosure and Standard & Poor's Register—Corporate.

> If you are a business or marketing researcher, you must be aware of the "D&B Report." This is the common term for a valuable report from D&B called the Business Information Report (BIR). This report includes directory information, a summary analysis, payment summary, financial summary, public filings, banking information, company history, and operations notes. For more information on this report, call D&B at 800-223-1026. The BIR is also available online on DIALOG (File 516) and NewsNet.

The results for this example show that CDP Technologies, Inc., is an electronic information-retrieval company specializing in the biomedical and health care markets. The company was started in 1985. It is located at 333 7th Avenue, 4th Floor, New York, NY 10001. The telephone number is 212-563-3006. The SIC code is 73 75 (Information Retrieval Services). Current sales are about $22 million, and the company employs about 100 people. The chief executive is Mark L. Nelson, president.

> From D&B files, you also find out the DUNS number. This unique identifier allows easy access to information throughout the D&B group of databases and publications.

Get the Latest *Wall Street Journal, Forbes, Fortune,* and Other Articles

To get current news, I start with Newspaper and Periodical Abstracts. Other sources include full-text newspapers, PR Newswire, Magazine Database, PTS New Products, Business Dateline, and Business Wire. By reading current news (1994 to 1995), you can find that on March 14, 1994, the company acquired BRS Online. You also find out that the company is changing its name to Ovid Technologies, Inc. Other recent articles include these:

- AMA chooses OVID full text to deliver journals; cites unique combination of searchability, full navigation, and graphical displays
  PR Newswire, May 9, 1995
- Busy times for CDP Technologies; company stresses convergence of technologies
  Tom Hogan, Information Today, Dec. 1994
- CDP Online offers pricing and interface options (new database service from CDP Technologies)
  Online, Nov.–Dec. 1994
- CDP Technologies commences public offering
  PR Newswire, June 17, 1994
- Good-bye BRS, hello CDP Online (BRS online service purchased by CDP Technologies)
  Tenopir, Carol
  Library Journal, March 1, 1995
- CDP Technologies changes name to Ovid Technologies, Inc.
  PR Newswire, May 2, 1995

Obtain Financial Information

For a publicly traded company, look up the annual report. I often use SEC Online, Moody's, Standard & Poor's, Disclosure, D&B, and others (for a private company, D&B is the best place to start). News reports also provide financials. A brief online review showed that Moody's Investors Services (April 25, 1995) had a CDP Technologies, Inc., annual report. In this case, I have also noted a few other news sources of interest:

- Digest of earnings reports
  Wall Street Journal (WSJ), Apr. 28, 1995

- CDP Technologies announces fourth quarter and annual results
PR Newswire, Feb. 13, 1995

Determine the Corporate Structure

Who owns the company? Who does the company own? Who are its subsidiaries? I often use Corporate Affiliations to answer these questions. For large, complex corporations, this database provides an understandable corporate hierarchy report. In this example, CDP has one subsidiary listed: CD Plus Ltd., in London.

Get Biographical Information and News Reports on Upper Management

Good management descriptions can be found in D&B and Standard & Poor's Register—Biographical. Other sources include newspapers, regional business journals, and biographical databases such as Who's Who and Bowker's. Here is a brief biographical sketch of CDP's CEO:

> *Mark L. Nelson was born in 1957. He graduated in 1981 Columbia University with a BA degree and obtained his MA degree in 1982. From 1982–84, he worked at Peat Marwick & Mitchell. From 1983–85, he was self employed and from 1985 on he has been at CDP Technologies Inc.*

Review the Company's Products and Determine Market Share or Get an Industry Overview

I use Trade and Industry Database, PROMT, and ABI/INFORM files as general-purpose, high-quality data sources. These databases are very comprehensive and are very well indexed, allowing efficient searching. (*Indexing* means that a person has reviewed the article, identified primary topics, and added index words to the database record.) Useful index words that apply to one or more of these databases are profiles (corporate and personal), industrywide conditions, company name, market share or shares, and product or industry names. In this example, I did a brief search using the company name as the search term, ensuring results that were about CDP Technologies. Additional articles were found with interim financial results and more product information.

Review Patent Holdings and Trademarks

In this example, I used Derwent World Patents Index and TRADEMARKSCAN. There are many other patent databases such as Claims, JAPIO, and U.S. Patents Fulltext. No recent patents were listed for CDP, but a trademark search showed that CDP Technologies, Inc., had registered "OVID" on October 25, 1994.

Read the Latest Investment Analysts' Reports

Find out what other people think of your competition. I used Investext, the major database of investment analysts' reports. Four reports were found that discussed CDP.

- CDP Technologies, Inc.—Company Report, May 3, '95, Market Guide Inc.
- CDP Technologies, Inc.—Company Report/March 31, '95, Market Guide Inc.
- FIserv, Inc.—Company Report, March 8, '95, Hambrecht & Quist
- CDP Technologies, Inc.—Company Report/March 8, '95, Market Guide Inc.

> Published investment and market analysis reports can be quite expensive. On DIALOG and other systems, a special output capability (called REPORT titles on DIALOG) allows the researcher inexpensively to review the titles and tables of contents of these reports. Then the researcher selects only the pages that are the most important, thus saving money.

LEXIS-NEXIS—EDGAR Plus

SEC filings provide large amounts of information on public corporations. LEXIS-NEXIS provides the EDGAR Plus file (published by Disclosure, Inc.) containing SEC filings received by the Electronic Data Gathering, Analysis, and Retrieval (EDGAR) System. It includes the following form types:

- 10-K from April 1993—comprehensive reports, including audited financial information, submitted annually. Figure 8-1 is a table of contents from a 10-K report.

- 10-Q from April 1993—quarterly reports without audited financials.

- Proxies from April 1993—submissions for a vote by security (stock) holders.

- 8-K from April 1993—released when significant changes occur.

- Registrations from November 1994—submitted when stock is issued.

Disclosure, Inc., has reformatted the tabular data and provided search, display, and print options.

For the example, I performed a search on *wireless* and *telecommunications* and *cellular* and *Japan* and *paging*. I retrieved twenty-two documents—SEC filings for companies that met the search criteria. The first ten results are listed here:

1. EDGAR Plus, PROVIDENCE JOURNAL CO, S-4 A00, DOCUMENT-DATE: April 5, 1995, FILING-DATE: April 5, 1995

2. EDGAR Plus, PEC ISRAEL ECONOMIC CORP, 10-K, DOCUMENT-DATE: December 31, 1994, FILING-DATE: April 1, 1995

3. EDGAR Plus, TIME WARNER INC, 10-K, DOCUMENT-DATE: December 31, 1994, FILING-DATE: March 31, 1995

4. EDGAR Plus, GLENAYRE TECHNOLOGIES INC, 10-K, DOCUMENT-DATE: December 31, 1994, FILING-DATE: March 29, 1995

5. EDGAR Plus, MOTOROLA INC, 10-K, DOCUMENT-DATE: December 31, 1994, FILING-DATE: March 24, 1995

6. EDGAR Plus, AIRTOUCH COMMUNICATIONS INC, 10-K, DOCUMENT-DATE: December 31, 1994, FILING-DATE: March 22, 1995

7. EDGAR Plus, AIRTOUCH COMMUNICATIONS INC, 10-K, Exhibit 13. Annual Report to Security Holders, Form 10-Q or Quarterly Report, FILING-DATE: March 22, 1995

8. EDGAR Plus, U S WEST INC, 10-K, Exhibit 13. Annual Report to Security Holders, Form 10-Q or Quarterly Report, FILING-DATE: March 8, 1995

9. EDGAR Plus, FIRST TRUST SPECIAL SITUATION TR SER 93, S-6 A00, DOCUMENT-DATE: December 8, 1994, FILING-DATE: December 8, 1994

10. EDGAR Plus, PACTEL CORP, 10-Q, DOCUMENT-DATE: September 30, 1994, FILING-DATE: November 11, 1994

```
ITEM 1.    Business

ITEM 2.    Properties

ITEM 3.    Legal Proceedings

ITEM 4.    Submission of Matters to a Vote of Security
           Holders


PART II

ITEM 5.    Market for Registrant's Common Equity and
           Related Stockholder Matters

ITEM 6.    Selected Financial Data

ITEM 7.    Management's Discussion and Analysis of
           Financial Condition and Results of Operations

ITEM 8.    Financial Statements and Supplementary Data

ITEM 9.    Changes in and Disagreements with Accountants
           on Accounting and Financial Disclosure


PART III

ITEM 10.   Directors and Executive Officers of the Reg-
           istrant

ITEM 11.   Executive Compensation

ITEM 12.   Security Ownership of Certain Beneficial Own-
           ers and Management

ITEM 13.   Certain Relationships and Related Trans-
           actions


PART IV

ITEM 14.   Exhibits, Financial Statement Schedules, and
           Reports on Form 8-K
```

Figure 8-1
What's in a 10-K report?

A Patent Search

Patents are one of the most important sources of technology information. Online, patent information is available from more than fifty-five countries and issuing authorities. Patent information is available for more than 10 million patents.

Patents provide an important insight to your competitors' technology and help you determine the potential competitive responses to your products. (The subset of market research that focuses on your competitors is called *Competitor Intelligence.*)

Historical data is quite complete online. Detailed abstracts and major claims of U.S. patents are available dating from 1950, and full text is available dating from 1974. In fact, for patents cited in patents issued after 1947, information goes back to 1790.

Patents are available in full text online, and full copies of patents are available by fax.

Some important terms to know when conducting preliminary patent research include:

- A *patent family* is all of the patent applications filed with all the various patent authorities for a single invention.

- A *patent citation* is a legally required note (written by the patent examiner) on a new patent application that indicates what prior art patents have been examined.

- *Patent publication* is the public release of a patent application or granted patent. While most countries publish patent applications, the United States publishes only granted patents.

Derwent (800-451-3451), a major provider of online patent information, suggests some useful patent analyses that are easily performed online for the patents in the industry or product area of interest. First is an analysis of widely protected patents. This is a ranking of patents by the number of countries where patents have been obtained. Patents of great commercial value are frequently patented in many countries.

Another valuable analysis is ranking new foreign patent publications. Companies rarely file patents outside their home country if the patent is not expected to be valuable. Therefore, lists of new foreign patent applications tend to show important patents in the field of interest.

Ranking of patents by the number of times they are cited provides a historical view of important patents. Note that companies that are strong here but have few newer patents may have lost their competitive edge or may be pulling out of a specific market.

Another Sample Search

An exercise from a DIALOG training class demonstrates the power of online patent searching in professional databases: "Find a patent with the US application number 214041. Then find related patents by using the classification code given on this patent."

This search was performed in a DIALOG ONTAP training database, CLAIMS(ONTAP) from IFI/Plenum Data Corp. The search was done by specifying the application number. The search retrieved a patent entitled M/WELL SAFETY VALVE, U.S. Patent No. 4376464. From the record I determined the classification number to be 166324000.

Now, a search was performed by specifying that classification number. Four patents were retrieved.

- M/WELL SAFETY VALVE—the original patent
- M/FLUID DISPLACEMENT WELL SAFETY VALVE
- M/PRESSURE BALANCED BALL VALVE DEVICE
- M/LUBRICATOR VALVE APPARATUS

This search demonstrates some of the capabilities of online patent searching. To learn more about this specialized field, it is best to take vendor-supplied training courses.

A Trademark Search

A trademark is a word, symbol, design, or other device that identifies particular products or services in the marketplace. Trademark research can be important when you are doing market research. You may need to look at trademarks to perform preliminary screening for your new marks, identify new products competitors may be planning, or find what company owns a specific mark. Trademarks may be searched by words, designs, owners, and slogans.

As an example, I looked for active United States trademarks containing the word *Internet.* I used TRADEMARKSCAN-US FED from Thomson & Thomson for this search and found 214 active trademarks. I then looked if any had been finalized in 1995 and found one: the INTERNET SERVICES CORPORATION, a company providing sales, training, and educational motivational subject matter for businessmen and entrepreneurs.

The Test Case

"We're thinking of selling a new product putting Global Positioning System (GPS) receivers in taxis so that taxi companies can track drivers and drivers can find locations. What can you tell me about this?"

This is a simple market research request that I will use as an example to demonstrate how to use online databases for marketing research. I will follow the basic search steps previously outlined in Chapter 5.

Define and Understand the Problem

Now is the time to ask questions to determine what information is really needed. In the real world, this could be a complex problem requiring an industry overview, a detailed listing of potential competitors, and so on. For the example, I will limit the information needed to the following:

1. Recent industry news. What's been written in papers and magazines?

2. A brief company overview of a major GPS manufacturer—Trimble Navigation.

3. A preliminary patent list.

Understand the Vocabulary of Your Problem

The next step is to generate a list of key words and phrases to use as search terms. By using a technical reference book and a magazine on GPS (*GPS World* from Advanstar Communications), I determined that the key terms for this search are *GPS* or *Global Positioning System; taxis* or *taxicabs; navigate* or *navigation* or *navigating* or *locate* or *location* or *locating;* and *track* or *tracking.* The news search is limited to this year and last year.

In this example, I specified the name of the manufacturer to profile. If you don't know the names of companies, remember to look up the SIC code. For "Search, Detection, Navigation, Guidance, Aeronautical and Nautical Systems and Instruments" manufacturers, the SIC code is 3812. Use of this code, along with the terms *GPS* or *Global Positioning Systems,* will find the companies of interest.

Determine Appropriate Sources

Knowledge of the available types of databases and their contents makes this task much easier—the advantage of the well-trained information professional. Determine what journals or newspapers report on your project area. Find online sources that include those journals or newspapers by using reference books or reference materials provided by database vendors and other authors.

Select and use sources that cover the topics of your search. For the brief company profile, I will use D&B Market Identifiers. For patents, I will use Derwent World Patent Index. For industry news in this example, I wanted business references and articles about high-technology businesses, so I chose these (from DIALOG):

- Databases that cover selected journals. As mentioned in Chapter 6, a powerful tool for picking databases that have full-text sources on your topic is BiblioData's *Fulltext Sources Online.* By looking there, I found that *Transportation Journal* is online in both ABI/INFORM and Trade & Industry Database and *Global Positioning & Navigation News* is available in PTS Newsletter (or Newsletter Database).

- Databases that are oriented toward high-technology business.

The databases I selected were the following:

- Trade & Industry Database, from Inform Access Company
- ABI/INFORM, from UMI
- PTS PROMT, from Information Access Company
- Magazine Database, from Information Access Company
- McGraw-Hill Publications Online, from McGraw-Hill
- PTS Newsletter DB, from Information Access Company
- Time Publications, from Time, Inc.

These databases all met the specified criteria. (They are a good starting point for many business searches.) I searched multiple databases because each covers a different selection of material. Sometimes one can use a single database, but using multiple databases reduces the chance of missing a critical piece of information.

Many other databases could also have been chosen, such as newspapers. For a comprehensive search, I frequently use more sources and more database services.

Create the Research Strategy

My research strategy to obtain both patent and news information is to select the search terms I generated in reviewing the vocabulary. On DIALOG, the search is written as follows:

(gps OR global(w)position?(w)system?) AND (taxi OR taxis OR taxicab?) AND (navigat? OR locat?) AND (track OR tracking)

where "?" is the truncation operator and "(w)" means adjacent in the specified order.

Go Online

Next, the search was run, using the specified search strategy, using the selected databases, and limiting to this year and last year. Twenty-three articles were found; the following were good ones (the other articles were purely aviation-related):

1. The digital traveler (multimedia products)
2. On the road again—with a digital map (consumer map software) (Buyer's Guide)
3. PDAs will usher in the next net revolution
4. Tibs may use satellite system for its buses. May launch automatic vehicle location sys utilizing U.S. Global Positioning System
5. Press a button on special terminals to order a taxi Introduces satellite-based radiophone system within next year
6. Agreeing to disagree
7. Surface attention
8. Year-end review: verticals remain slow, but smrs show promise; omnitracs booms
9. Real men don't ask directions (includes related articles)
10. GPS test; five leading aviation hand-helds go head-to-head (global positioning system)
11. On-Road, On-Time, and On-Line: A trucking firm finds a combination of trucks, GPS technology, and computers pays off in fleet flexibility and control

12. GPS AND THE NATIONAL AIRSPACE SYSTEM:
    Here's what you can do with GPS now and in the future.

The directory search found that Trimble's full name is Trimble Navigation Limited, Inc., and that the firm is located at 585 N. Mary Avenue, Sunnyvale, CA 94086-2931. Its business is manufacturing electronic navigation instruments. Trimble was formed in 1978 and incorporated in 1981. Annual sales are approximately $150 million. Trimble has about 830 employees. The president and CEO is Charles R. Trimble.

The final search task was a quick review of patents. I used the Derwent World Patent Index (1981 on) for this and ran the same search as the first. There were 85,173 patents about "(gps OR global(w)position?(w)system?)" and 12 patents about GPS and taxicabs. The complete search statement found 5 interesting patents:

1. Communication procedure between clients and taxi firms drivers—using expert system and geographical *location* system to select nearest taxi to client according to past and present traffic parameters

2. Occupant attack alarm system for taxis and other motor vehicles—alerts control center or police by automatic radio emergency calls and position transmissions of which assailant is unaware

3. Navigation device using global positioning system satellites—provides position measurement using GPS signals, displays position of vehicle concerned and communicates with other surface vehicles

4. Automatic vehicle location (AVL) system—includes vehicle-mounted RX-TX units and base station all receiving signals from GPS satellites

5. Vehicle tracking system, partic. for refuse truck—tracks vehicle location and loading-unloading times

Refine the Search

Remember that searching is interactive. Improve your results by modifying your strategy as you go. The next step is to learn from the results and modify the search. One thing you immediately learn from this search is that with *GPS* and *taxi,* you retrieve airplane-related articles. However, one article, primarily about airplanes, had a short informative sidebar about our exact topic. It would be unwise to modify the search by adding "NOT airplane?"

In this example, I reviewed the search results (titles) by eye and rejected eleven of twenty-three. A straightforward way to improve the results is to download the articles of interest and read them. By reading the articles, you can improve your search vocabulary and search terms. Perhaps there is a newly coined term that exactly describes the area of interest; use it and repeat the search.

Look at the best articles and review the index terms associated with those documents; then rerun the search using those index terms. Look at all the companies mentioned; then expand the search by adding articles about those companies.

Depending on the results, there are many ways to expand or limit the original search. If I had received no useful results, I could have searched additional years or added more databases. If I had received too many results, I could have limited the search further by requiring that my search terms appear in the titles of documents or by reducing the number of years searched.

Patent searches can also be easily modified from experience. By reviewing the interesting patents, the researcher can identify companies, inventors, classification codes, index terms, and other things to enhance the search.

Collect and Report Results

Once you have a set of documents you want, you can get output many different ways, depending on the database and system. Some of these ways are:

1. Download full text to your computer—the fastest way. However, most downloaded information is text only: graphs, pictures, and some tables are not available. This

situation is improving with the increasing availability of image files that contain all the graphics information as well as the text.

2. Have documents E-mailed, mailed, or faxed to you.

3. Find them in the library.

An Alternative Search: Using TARGET from DIALOG

TARGET is a relevance search tool from DIALOG that provides outputs based on the number of occurrences and locations of search terms. It is best applied to searching in full-text databases and, by default, limits results to the top fifty items from this year and last year. Here are the formats for TARGET inputs:

- All search terms are on a single line separated by spaces.
- Phrases are enclosed in single quotes.
- Synonyms or like terms are in parentheses.
- Truncation is used (with "?").
- Mandatory terms are marked with an asterisk.

I repeated the news search from before using the same databases with TARGET. The TARGET search request looked like this:

```
*( gps 'global position? system?') ( taxi taxis taxicab?) ( navigat?
locat? track?)
```

This search returned thirty-eight articles, of which twenty-three were different from those found in the command search. Of the new articles, twelve appeared worthy of further review. They are listed here:

1. Future mapping (overview of market for global positioning systems and geographic information systems) (Forward Spin) (PC Week Inside)

2. Tokyo Motor Show (Editorial)

3. New radiophone cab system to make its debut next year. Joins with SBS Taxi to introduce radiophone paging system to track taxis in 1995

4. Products, Services & Technology Corp. announces financial results.

5. ACCQPOINT offers wide area differential GPS services throughout North America.

6. Smart cars guide Chicago drivers; ADVANCE navigation system will relay traffic information to 4,000 vehicles.

7. Navigation #2: Dynaguide To Go Through Further Tests As Launch Date Is Put Back To May

8. Collins extends Mode S applications.

9. Charting new directions into the bookstores; maps on disk make the first inroads into booksellers' shelves (includes related information on mapping software companies)

10. Herbert A. Simon (artificial intelligence pioneer) (Interview)

11. Cellular/vehicle navigation tests portend new European markets.

12. Cue Announces International Paging And Differential GPS Services In Singapore.

I have found that this result of comparable, but not overlapping, retrievals to be common with a combined use of a relevance search and a command search. The best results come from combining the two search methods for many types of searches, particularly those searches with large numbers of hits.

This total search (three parts) cost about $75 and took about twenty-five minutes online.

Summary

In this chapter, I have demonstrated the use of the professional information services for market research by performing simple, illustrative searches. In Chapters 11 and 14, the Test Case search will be repeated to allow some direct comparisons of the various information services.

For Further Reading

I am not suggesting specific books here, but I am suggesting that you take advantage of the many manuals and other documentation available from both database publishers and producers. Call your online vendor and ask. I, like most other information professionals, maintain a library of up-to-date database documentation.

9 | *The Internet*

The next three chapters will discuss the Internet and its uses for secondary marketing research. This book is not intended as a Yellow Pages for the Internet: though resource locations are identified and used for examples, no effort to provide a comprehensive list has been made. Things change so fast that there is no guarantee that any resource location will be the same when you read this book.

> The perfect resource I found yesterday is gone or moved today. As an information professional, I spend a lot of time keeping up. My methods and tools are described in Chapter 15.

This chapter is a brief introduction to the Internet and to business use of the Internet. It focuses on research uses and introduces tools for research. It presents some of the popular myths of the Internet and tries to address the reality behind the myths. Dealing with and understanding the information available via the Internet is necessary for the information professional and may be useful to the secondary marketing researcher. Currently, useful material is hard to find on the Internet. Beginners on the Internet should read one or more of the books listed at the end of the chapter.

The Hope of the Future

According to the articles that bombard us daily, the Internet is the future. To many people, when one mentions computers or online, their first thought is "the Internet." It is used by a very large number of people and organizations, including students, newspapers, governments, hobbyists, academics, businesses, publishers, and librarians. The largest use is E-mail—it connects people efficiently throughout the world.

According to an Internet Domain Survey performed by Network Wizards (http://www.nw.com), the number of Internet hosts has grown from 1,313,000 in January 1993 to 4,852,000 in January 1995. The number of domains has grown from 21,000 to 71,000 in the same time frame.

The most common types of information currently available on the Internet are government documents, works with expired copyrights, works that are in the public domain, and works that authors are making freely available to the Internet community. Types of information you are unlikely to find include commercial works protected by copyright law.

Businesses are using the Internet more and more. They use it for E-mail and they use it for commerce. As the issue of security is resolved, business use for commercial transactions will continue to increase. Public relations information, company announcements, and technical material from many corporations are becoming widely available. More and more businesses are using the Web as an electronic promotional brochure. As this trend continues, and as search tools get better, the Web will become more valuable to the market researcher.

One important business impact of the Internet is the launching of a major publishing boom. Many books have been written on topics related to the Internet. A quick search of the online database Books in Print (R.R. Bowker, New York) found 230 books with *Internet* in the title! A list of those titles that are business-oriented, along with detailed references for the books I use, is included at the end of the chapter.

The Internet does have some legal requirements and issues. Parts of the Internet are subsidized by federal agencies and are to be used for government, research, and education purposes. On those subsidized parts, commercial activities are not allowed (activities such as accounting, billing, or marketing). Commercial activities use unsubsidized parts of the net, and access costs more.

Copyright and import/export legal issues are discussed in Chapter 18.

What Is the Internet?

The Internet is a network interlinking other networks. It is also a client/server system. The connection or interlink protocol is named the Transmission Control Protocol/ Internet Protocol, commonly called TCP/IP. It is a packet-switched network—information is transmitted in small packets. Each packet includes data along with source and destination information. These small packets are transmitted independently and may take different routes from sender to receiver. At the destination, using data contained within the individual packets, the information is reassembled. This sounds complicated, but luckily the process is transparent to the user.

The Internet started small as a government project called ARPANET in 1969. By 1982, it contained about twenty-five active networks and a few hundred computer sites (or hosts). Now it has more than 13,000 active networks and more than 4 million hosts.

Any computer connected directly to the Internet can be a client, a server, or both. Your computer's status will depend on the type of software you install and use. For marketing research and general Internet purposes, I use client software to access information on other computers—servers. For example, on my computer, I have installed a World Wide Web (WWW) client (called a browser), a Gopher client, a File Transfer Protocol (FTP) client, a Telnet client, and a mail reader.

The Internet and its tools are described by many new phrases and acronyms. See the box for a brief glossary.

The Internet Has a Whole New Vocabulary

ARPANET: the predecessor to the Internet, which was started in 1969 with funds from the Defense Department's Advanced Research Projects Agency.

ASCII: a universal computer code for English letters and characters.

backbone: a high-speed network that connects several computers.

baud: the speed at which modems transfer data. One baud is roughly equal to one bit per second.

Client: a program that requests services from another computer.

domain name: a multipart name that identifies an Internet computer.

download: to copy a file from another system to your computer.

E-mail: electronic mail. Used as both a noun and a verb.

FAQ: Frequently Asked Questions. An FAQ file is a compilation of answers to such questions.

flame: online yelling and/or ranting directed at somebody else.

freeware: software that is released for anyone to use at no charge.

FTP: File Transfer Protocol. A system for transferring files across the Net.

Gateway: a computer that interconnects one network to another.

GIF: Graphic Interchange Format. A common format for transferring graphics.

HTTP: HyperText Transfer Protocol. A protocol for describing Web pages so they may be displayed on many different types of computer.

IP address: an Internet address expressed in numbers.

Listserv: a program that automatically responds to and distributes E-mail messages.

log off: to disconnect.

log on/log in: to connect to the Net.

mailing list: a group discussion in which messages are delivered right to your mailbox, instead of to a newsgroup.

network: a communications system that links two or more computers.

NIC: Network Information Center.

NSF: National Science Foundation. It funds NSFNet, a high-speed network that once formed the backbone of the Internet in the United States.

offline: when your computer is not connected to the Net, you are offline.

online: when your computer is connected to the Net, you are online.

post: to compose a message for a newsgroup and then send it out for others to see.

PPP: Point to Point Protocol. A protocol for exchanging Internet information over a phone line.

prompt: when another computer asks you to do something and waits for you to respond. For example, if you see "login:" it means that you should type your user name.

protocol: a method used to transfer a file between a host system and your computer. There are several types, such as Kermit, YMODEM, and ZMODEM. Also the method used for computers to talk to one another on the Net—TCP/IP.

README files: files found on computer sites or shipped with programs and that provide explanations and helpful information.

RFC: Request for Comments—a series of documents that describe various technical aspects of the Internet.

screen capture: capturing what is visible on the screen to a file.

server: a computer that can distribute information or files automatically in response to specific requests.

shareware: try-before-you-buy software. Freely available on the Net. If you like and use the software, you then pay for it.

TCP/IP: Transmission Control Protocol/Internet Protocol. The particular method of transferring information over the Internet.

Telnet: a program that lets you connect (log on) to other computers on the Internet.

upload: to copy a file from your computer to another system.

All computers connected directly to the Internet have their own address. Addresses are described in two ways. An Internet Protocol (IP) address is a set of four numbers separated by periods: 194.90.151.1. Originally this was the only address system. Obviously, these addresses are hard to remember. The Domain Name System (DNS), developed by Paul Mockapetris in 1984, provides more user-friendly alphanumeric names, such as my E-mail address: jfl@vivamus.com.

Jfl@vivamus.com—*jfl* is my user name, *vivamus* is the organization name, and *com* is the top-level domain indicating a commercial site.

The Internet Assigned Numbers Authority has overall responsibility for addresses; the Internet Registry manages day-to-day operations. These unique addresses—IP or DNS— are the equivalent of a telephone number or mailing address. Some top-level domains (the ones at the far right of the domain name) are shown in Table 9-1.

Table 9-1
Top-Level Internet Domains

Domain	Organization
com	Commercial and industrial organizations
edu	Universities and other educational organizations
gov	Government
mil	Military or defense organizations
net, org	Network operation and service organizations
us, uk, ca, au (etc.)	Geographical domain

For example, my domain name is vivamus.com, a commercial site.

The Internet is growing and changing rapidly, so any statistics and demographics are both approximate and immediately out of date. Here are some typical Internet facts from 1994:

- The growth rate is about 5 percent per month.
- From a marketing standpoint, Internet users have positive demographics for many products. They are predominantly highly educated, young, male, and well paid.
- It is becoming more international in nature, with about one-third of the networks from outside the United States.
- E-mail is the service used by the most people.
- File transfers (using File Transfer Protocol—FTP) create the highest volume of traffic.
- The World Wide Web (WWW or simply the Web) and Gopher combined are the fastest-growing segment.
- It is becoming more commercial, with most new commercial activity appearing on the WWW.

Access

There are three main types of access to the Internet available for a private computer (over a phone line using a modem) from an Internet access provider. One is a true connection, in which your computer is actually connected to the Internet and your computer acts as a client. This type of connection is commonly available as a SLIP or PPP account. You will want this type of account to use the World Wide Web. SLIP is the Serial Line Internet Protocol, a type of modem connection used to emulate a TCP/IP connection with an Internet server. PPP is a similar connection that is also suitable.

The other typical connection readily available is a shell account. This is a user account on a computer that is connected to the Internet. Basically, you provide directions to that computer to perform client services on the Internet. It performs actions for you and stores the results. You then download results to your computer. Commands are frequently transmitted using UNIX, a relatively unfriendly but powerful language used by most Internet computers. Even if you have a direct (PPP or SLIP) account, you will also want a shell account, to use in case of a problem with the direct connection. Many providers offer a shell account automatically with a PPP or SLIP connection. Shell accounts also allow you to perform UNIX tasks on your own files on the provider's computer if that should become necessary.

A larger company may have a more direct connection, with high-speed phone lines and internal interconnections via a local area network. If your company or facility has this, contact your information services department.

Don't worry too much about all this complexity. Your service provider will help with the setup, and many instructional books are available. Commercial software makers now provide in a single box all the software you need to set up a fully functional Internet client.

The major consumer databases have or are getting full access to the Internet. Web browsers from AOL, Prodigy, and CompuServe work reasonably well. If you don't use the Internet a lot, one of those services would be suitable.

It's Not Free—But How Much Does It Cost?

One of the most common Internet myths is "It's free!" This leads to the myth that information found on the Internet is free. It comes as a great shock to many people that neither access to the Internet nor all the information found on the Internet is free. For example, one vendor's prices (as of April 1995) were the following (excluding hourly charges):

UNIX Shell Account	$19.50/month
SLIP or PPP, 40 hours allotted	$29/month
Slip or PPP, unlimited hours	$79/month
Digital data path (57.6K)	$495/month

Although prices vary, these are not unusual. As you can see, the Internet certainly is not free.

Another price issue is the cost of a phone call. Business and long-distance connections that charge by the minute may add greatly to the cost of Internet access. Very high speed lines such as ISDN have significant monthly and usage charges also. Of course, you need a computer and modem as well.

The belief that the Internet is free probably comes from the fact that most users had their first Internet contact via computers belonging to a university, a library, or other large organization. In such systems, the actual costs were not passed down to individual users. Another factor is that Internet vendors frequently have no per-hour charges: once you have paid your monthly bill, no further charges for usage occur. (In some areas, you may find free-nets—this means that someone else is paying.)

It is important to select an Internet service provider carefully. You need a provider who can best meet all of your requirements. Lists of vendors can be obtained from schools, magazines, newspapers, local computer groups, and books. You should ask prospective service providers for information regarding

- The type of access they offer.
- Their monthly charges.
- Service availability.
- The number of telephone lines.
- The disk space allotted.
- Support.
- Free software availability. Very good Internet software is available as freeware or shareware.

Information is not free either! Though there is a lot of public domain information on the Internet that is legally free, copyrighted information is still copyrighted, and the copyright holder is entitled to payment. Public domain information is frequently of little value to the market researcher.

New for-fee sites are appearing on the Internet every day. The pricing plans are still evolving, but there appears to be a per-transaction model instead of a connect-time model. (New professional services are also moving to the transaction price model.) In the transaction price model, the only time a fee is paid is when a document or article is accessed or downloaded. Copyright in cyberspace is a legal area in turmoil at present.

The Big Story—The World Wide Web

The World Wide Web may be the application that brings the Internet to everyone. The Web is extremely easy to use. It is also easy to publish on the Web. As a consequence, the Web is growing very fast and most new information is appearing on the Web. The growth of the Web has been astounding: although estimates vary widely, in 1994 about 300 new Web servers per month were added. By May 1995, Sun Microsystems (a major supplier of Internet servers) estimated that there were greater than 27,000 sites and that the number of sites was doubling every fifty-three days.

The World Wide Web is a hypertext system, which means that you can leap easily from point to point. With "browser" software such as Mosaic, an attractive graphical interface allows you to point and click your way. One minute you are reading a document located on a server at MIT in Cambridge, and the next you are reviewing a related graphic located on a server in Japan. This hypertext system is made up of documents (or information sites) connected by links or pointers to other electronic locations. The protocol for the Web is the HyperText Transfer Protocol (HTTP).

Each document on the Web has a specific electronic address, called a Uniform Resource Locator (URL). In many documents, you will probably notice that certain key words, phrases, or items in lists are highlighted in a different color. When you click your mouse on the highlighted item or graphic, your browser software reads the associated URL and connects you to the remote computer home of the associated document. This software capability makes finding documents on the Web relatively easy.

The URL format is straightforward and easy to use. The basic format is scheme://host.port/path, where

- **scheme** is the retrieval methodology or protocol, such as "http" for a Web document, "ftp" for FTP access, "gopher" for gopherspace, and "telnet" for Telnet access.
- **host** is the computer where service resides.

- **port** is the service identifier.
- **path** is the location of a resource on a particular computer host.

The Web was born in Switzerland in March 1989. A physicist, Tim Berners-Lee of the European Particle Physics Laboratory (CERN), wanted to be able to exchange information rapidly among geographically separated members of his scientific community. He proposed a hypertext system, where key words or phrases in a given document could be linked to other documents. By January 1993 there were fifty Web servers in existence.

Explosive growth began with the development and general release in 1993 of the Mosaic Web browser. Mosaic was developed by Marc Andreeson at the National Center for Supercomputing Applications (NCSA) at the University of Illinois, Champaign-Urbana. Versions of NCSA Mosaic were released for X Windows (UNIX), Microsoft Windows 3.1, and the Macintosh.

New browsers, including many commercial versions, have been released, and "home pages" (a name for a Web site) have proliferated. Figure 9-1 shows a typical home page.

A marketing researcher or professional searcher need not know about the actual protocol for creating a Web page or document. I will give only a very brief introduction here.

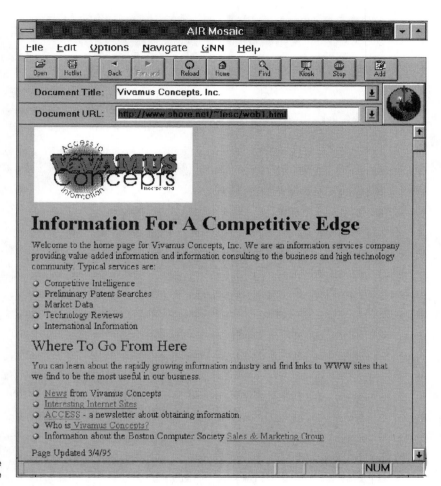

Figure 9-1
A typical World Wide
Web home page

Documents for the Web are written in HyperText Markup Language (HTML). HTML is a collection of styles (indicated by markup tags) that define the various components of a World Wide Web document. Figure 9-2 shows the HTML for the page shown in Figure 9-1. Some basic markup tags used in HTML are the following:

- Title—<title> *title text* </title>—A title is generally displayed in the title box of the browser.

```
<html>
<head>
<title>Vivamus Concepts, Inc.</title>
</head>
<body>
<img src=s_logo.gif ALT="Vivamus Concepts, Inc., Access to Information">
<h1><b>Information For A Competitive
Edge<strong></strong></b></h1><p><p>
```

Welcome to the home page for Vivamus Concepts, Inc. We are an information services company providing value added information and information consulting to the business and high technology community. Typical services are:<p>

```
<ul>
<li>Competitive Intelligence
<li>Preliminary Patent Searches
<li>Market Data
<li>Technology Reviews
<li>International Information
</ul>
<p>
<h3>Where To Go From Here</h3><p>
```

You can learn about the rapidly growing information industry and find links to Internet sites that we find to be the most useful in our business.<p><p>

```
<ul>
<li><a href="vcnews.html">News</a> from Vivamus Concepts.
<li><a href="sstindex.html">Internet sites</a> we use for business (and
pleasure).
<li><a href="access.html">ACCESS</a>—our newsletter about obtaining
information.
<li>More information about <a href="vcview.html">Vivamus Concepts</a>
and the services we provide.
<li>Information about the Boston Computer Society <a href="bcssm.html">
Sales and Marketing Group</a>
<li>Read about <a href="infone.html">Information New England</a>—an
informal organization of people in the information industry.
</ul>
<p>Page Updated 3/15/95<p>
```

Contact John Lescher with questions or comments at 1-800-903-9939 or jfl@vivamus.com<p>

http://www.shore.net/~lesc/web1.html<p>

```
</body>
</html>
```

Figure 9-2
The HyperText Markup
Language (HTML) code
used for the example
home page

- Headings—<h#> heading text </h#>—HTML has six levels of headings, numbered 1 through 6, with 1 being the most prominent. Headings are displayed in larger and/or bolder fonts than normal body text.
- Paragraphs—<p>—A Web browser ignores line breaks and starts a new paragraph only when it reaches a <p> tag.
- Links—The power of HTML comes from its ability to link text or images to another document. The browser highlights these regions (usually with color and/or underlines) to indicate that they are hypertext links. An example link to *NCSA's Beginner's Guide to HTML* is

<a href="http://www.ncsa.uiuc.edu/General/Internet/WWW/HTMLPrimer.html">A Beginner's Guide to HTML</a>

The Web is not perfect. It is frequently slow. Authors often choose beauty over content—does everyone need huge graphics that dramatically slow transfer rates? Like the rest of the Internet, it is not well organized, and search tools are in their infancy.

Other Internet Tools

Although the World Wide Web gets most of the current attention, there are other tools to access information on the Internet. They include FTP, Gopher, Telnet, ARCHIE, Veronica, WAIS, and mailing lists. These are discussed next. If you have a SLIP or PPP connection, client software for these applications resides on your computer; if you have a UNIX shell connection, the client software resides on the host computer.

File Transfer Protocol

You can access an FTP server, a computer on the Internet set up to offer information to other Internet users via FTP.

FTP enables you to download files (copy files from the FTP server to your computer) or upload files (copy files from your computer to the FTP server). Most FTP servers allow anonymous login; sites that do so require you to enter a password. Although almost any password will work, most sites prefer that you enter your E-mail address so they can track who is accessing their files. Once connected, you can choose files that you want transferred to you or from you to the other party. There must be an FTP client on one end (your computer) and an FTP server at the other end of each connection.

Most directories (a list of the files stored in the computer) that you access will have a special file called an index file. You can open this file to learn what information is contained in each file on that particular server. Modern client software makes FTP very easy to use.

Gopher

Gopher is a program that provides easy access to Internet-based online databases and services by allowing you to make selections from a menu. You can also copy text files and programs. Gopher is so called because it can "go for" information and because it was developed at the University of Minnesota, home of the Golden Gophers. A Gopher server is a computer system resident on the Internet that services the information requests issued by Gopher client programs. When you access a Gopher server, you get a search menu—a numbered list. You select a number to retrieve a document or to connect to another server. An example of a Gopher list is shown in Figure 9-3. The Gopher services on the Internet are very popular because they are very easy to use and learn. As a result, they may sometimes be crowded and slow.

```
Root gopher server: gopher.micro.umn.edu
-->  1. Information About Gopher/
     2. Computer Information/
     3. Discussion Groups/
     4. Fun & Games/
     5. Internet file server (ftp) sites/
     6. Libraries/
     7. News/
     8. Other Gopher and Information Servers/
     9. Phone Books/
    10. Search lots of places at the U of M <?>
    11. University of Minnesota Campus Information/
```

Figure 9-3
A sample Gopher menu

Telnet

One of the most useful facilities of the Internet is Telnet.
The Telnet function provides a method of making your computer a terminal on any Telnet-compatible computer on the
Internet. Using Telnet, you log onto a remote computer and
use software, access files, and execute programs. Libraries of
information and huge databases of research material can be
accessed through Telnet. I frequently use Telnet to access
local public- and university-library catalogs.

Another common use of Telnet is for users to log into their
own computers from remote locations. In this case, users
enter their own user names and passwords and, therefore,
have the same user privileges they would have when logged
in without using Telnet. Telnet allows you to log onto other
services through your Internet connection. For example, you
can log onto DIALOG and CompuServe.

In order to establish a Telnet connection, you need to know
the name of the computer site you want to access and have a
valid user name and password for that site. Accessing a Tel-

net site generally requires that your communications software emulate a VT100 terminal, a standard computer terminal emulation that is commonly available in most computer communication programs. Some Telnet sites allow guest logins. Guest accounts typically are restricted to limited types of actions during a Telnet session. Just type "guest" at the user id prompt. In most circumstances you do not have to enter a password if you are a guest. Sometimes descriptive text seen when logging onto a Telnet site indicates the user id and password to be used by visitors. Keep in mind that not all Telnet sites allow guest access. For some sites you must have a password. Passwords are generally available to members of the organization providing the site.

Performance at Telnet sites is affected by both Internet usage and local demand. During heavy usage, performance will deteriorate quickly. Many times, the most popular host computers on the Internet are very busy and won't even permit you to log on.

Internet Mailing Lists

Mailing lists and Usenet newsgroups are other ways to access information on the Internet. Unlike E-mail, which is usually "one to one," these services are "many to many." These are the discussion groups or forums of the Internet. Here you can read opinions on a tremendous variety of topics. You can post questions and receive answers. For example, by posting a request to a mailing list, I obtained the names of several experts in a selected field.

There are mailing lists and newsgroups on about any subject imaginable—and the number is growing all the time. The organization of newsgroups is hierarchical, with the first field being the broadest heading or category. Additional fields provide subcategories. Table 9-2 lists the first fields in use.

Table 9-2 Internet Newsgroup Categories		
	alt	Alternative or nonmainstream, often bizarre or offensive to some
	bionet	Biology, mostly academic and professional
	bit	Bitnet "listserv" groups
	biz	Business, including commercial advertising
	comp	Computer technology
	de	In German language
	fj	In Japanese language
	ieee	Institute of Electronic and Electrical Engineers
	gnu	Free Software Foundation's "GNU" project
	k12	Primary and secondary education
	misc	Unclassifiable under a single heading listed here
	news	News network and news software
	rec	Hobbies, recreation, arts (virtually everything imaginable)
	sci	Sciences (natural, social, technological)
	soc	Social issues
	talk	Debate and controversy

How to Find Things

"Finding things on the Internet is hard . . . this may not seem like earth shattering news to anyone who has been on the Net for more than a few days."

—P. Deutsch, *Internet World*, May 1994

Finding the services or information you need on the Internet is not easy. Sheer size and rate of change are the problems. Search tools exist, and although these tools are getting better, they are still relatively poor. A brief overview of the more important search tools is provided here. The best way to really use these tools is to get one of the recommended books, get online, and try them.

ARCHIE

ARCHIE is a program that lets you type in a search word to find files that are stored on FTP servers. Alan Emtage, Bill Heelan, and Peter Deutsch, students at McGill University in Montreal, created the database system called ARCHIE that periodically calls up file libraries and finds out what is available. FTP sites are regularly indexed by title and keyword and ARCHIE searches these indexes. ARCHIE is a good tool to use when searching for software or documents.

FTP, when used in conjunction with ARCHIE, can search thousands of databases all over the world for the file or files that contain desired information. A researcher can Telnet to an ARCHIE server (log in with user name "ARCHIE"), type in a file name, and locate it on the Net. At the time of writing, ARCHIE catalogs about 1000 file libraries around the world. Table 9-3 lists some sites where ARCHIE is available.

I use ARCHIE by two means: by Telnet or by an ARCHIE client program on my host system. For Telnet, I go to an ARCHIE site (see Table 9-3) and log on as "archie." After I connect, the search request is "prog filename," where "filename" is the program or file I'm looking for. (Partial names are useful. But no wild cards are allowed.)

On a local ARCHIE client, the search procedure is simple:

1. Select ARCHIE from the Gopher menu.
2. Type in a search string relating to the desired files.
3. Receive the result—a list of locations where the files are available. (Returned in my case as a Gopher menu.)

Site	Address	Location
archie.uqam.ca*	132.208.250.10	Canada
archie.th-darmstadt.de*	130.83.22.60	Germany
archie.wide.ad.jp	133.4.3.6	Japan
archie.switch.ch*	130.59.1.40	Switzerland
archie.doc.ic.ac.uk*	146.169.11.3	United Kingdom
archie.unl.edu	129.93.1.14	USA (NE)
archie.rutgers.edu*	128.6.18.15	USA (NJ)
archie.internic.net*	198.48.45.10	USA (NJ)
archie.ans.net*	147.225.1.10	USA (NY)
archie.sura.net*	128.167.254.179	USA (MD)

Table 9-3
Internet ARCHIE Sites

VERONICA

VERONICA, developed at the University of Nevada at Reno by Steve Foster and Fred Barrie, does for gopherspace what ARCHIE does for FTP sites. Gopher is best used with a Gopher search program like VERONICA because Gopher itself is merely a way to list information in an organized fashion. VERONICA is a good tool for finding documents.

In most gophers, you access VERONICA by selecting "Other gopher and information services" at the main menu and then selecting "Search through gopherspace using VERONICA." Make that selection and a menu appears (Figure 9-4). If you already know where your information is (for example, a DOS program would often be located in a directory containing MS-DOS programs), do a directory-title search. Otherwise, do a general gopherspace search. VERONICA searches for text that appears in Gopher menus. The search procedure is straightforward:

1. Select VERONICA from the Gopher menu.
2. Type in a search string relating to the desired document(s).

```
-->   1. Search titles in Gopherspace using veronica .
      2. FAQ: Frequently-Asked Questions about veronica
         (1993/08/23).
      3. How to compose veronica queries (NEW June 24) READ
         ME!!.
      4. Search Gopher Directory Titles at PSINet <?>
      5. Search Gopher Directory Titles at SUNET <?>
      6. Search Gopher Directory Titles at U. of Manitoba <?>
      7. Search Gopher Directory Titles at University of
         Cologne <?>
      8. Search gopherspace at PSINet <?>
      9. Search gopherspace at SUNET <?>
     10. Search gopherspace at U. of Manitoba <?>
     11. Search gopherspace at University of Cologne <?>


Press ? for Help, q to Quit, u to go up a menu Page: 1/1
```

Figure 9-4
An Internet VERONICA
menu

3. See the results of the search returned as a Gopher menu.

4. Select a Gopher site from that menu.

Wide Area Information Servers

The Wide Area Information Server (WAIS) is a program that can search multiple databases in one search. It is a common-interface search tool—the user sees only one interface: the program worries about how to access information on the different databases. WAIS is full-text indexing software that's used to index large text files, documents, and periodicals.

You give WAIS a word and it scours the Net looking for places where it's mentioned. You can search WAIS indexes for everything from the text of the NAFTA treaty to information on Zen Buddhism. The output is a list of documents, each ranked according to how relevant to your search the WAIS thinks it is.

WAIS client programs can be found on many public-access Internet sites. If your home system has a WAIS client program, type "swais" at the command prompt and hit Enter. (The *s* stands for *simple.*) A good place to start is the University of Minnesota Gopher that lists all WAIS servers, both by location and by topic, at gophergw.micro.umn.edu. You can also Telnet to bbs.oit.unc.edu, which is run by the University of North Carolina. At the "login:" prompt, type "bbs" and hit Enter. First, tell the WAIS program which databases you want searched. Then select the desired keywords, hit Enter, and the search begins. The system returns a list of documents that match your search criteria.

Web Tools

I list here some of the search tools available for the World Wide Web. The World Wide Web is very valuable to secondary marketing research because of

- its growing importance,
- the number of business sites appearing, and
- the ability to access gopherspace and other Internet areas from a single, user-friendly interface.

Two primary types of search tools are available for the Web: manual indexes (a list you use like an index to a book) and automatically created, searchable databases (which you search by inputting keywords). Some of these tools, such as InfoSeek, are commercial sites. See Table 9-4.

Table 9-4
Web Search Tools

Manual Indexes	Databases Searchable by Keyword
Yahoo—http://akebono/stanford.edu/yahoo	InfoSeek—http://www.infoseek.com
EINET Galaxy—http://galaxy.einet.net/galaxy	Lycos—http://lycos.cs.cmu.edu
WWW Virtual Library—http://info.cern.ch/ hypertext/data_sources/by_subject	WWW Worm—http://www.cs.colorado/edu/ hume/nycybryan
Internet Yellow Pages— http://www.yellow.com	WebCrawler—http://www.biotech.washington.edu/ WebCrawler/WebQuery.html
	The Web Of Wonder—http://www.digimark.net

More information on Web searching appears in Chapter 11.

Summary

In this chapter I have looked at what the Internet is, how it is changing, and how it impacts secondary marketing researchers. The World Wide Web and various search tools for use on the Internet were discussed. The Internet has great potential, but it is not the best online resource for secondary marketing research—yet. It contains a large collection of business information, but you cannot search it efficiently. It is, however, very valuable in providing rapid access to renowned consultants and academic experts.

The next chapter is a more detailed review of the information available on the Internet. It also provides selected market research examples using the World Wide Web.

For Further Reading

1. *The Internet Companion,* second edition, by Tracey LaQuey (Addison-Wesley, 1994). One of the best introductory books to the Internet. A good place to start that won't overwhelm you.

2. *UNIX for Dummies,* by John R. Levine and Margaret Levine Young (IDG Books, 1993). If you need to use UNIX (and you will if you use a shell program), this book is a good starting spot.

3. *The Complete Idiot's Guide to the Internet,* by Peter Kent (Alpha Books, 1994). Ignore the terrible name. This book is a very readable and useful beginner's guide.

4. *The Internet Guide for New Users,* by Daniel P. Dern (McGraw-Hill, 1994). A classic and very good book—buy it!

5. *The World Wide Web Unleashed,* by John December and Neil Randall (SAMS Publishing, 1994). A fat book with lots of general information on the Web.

6. *Internet World,* a magazine published by Meckler Corp. E-mail: meckler@jvnc.net. Phone: 800-MECKLER. Worth reading every month.

7. *Online Access,* a magazine published by Chicago Fine Print. E-mail: 70324.343@compuserve.com. Another magazine with extensive Internet coverage worth reading.

8. *Teach Yourself Web Publishing with HTML in a Week,* by Laura Lemay (SAMS, 1995). If you want to create your own home page, buy it. No other book on Web authoring is a better place to start.

9. *Zen and the Art of the Internet: A Beginner's Guide to the Internet,* by Brendan Kehoe. One of the best books about the Internet is available for free online—for example at emoryu1.cc.emory.edu in the /computing/reference/networking/internet directory, or in the Internet Center on AOL.

10. *The Whole Internet User's Guide,* by Ed Krol. Another very good Internet book. (It's furnished in a special edition as the user's manual for Internet in a Box from Spry.) The book is published by O'Reilly and Associates, 800-998-9938.

Internet Business Titles Not Referenced Elsewhere

1. *A Tutorial on Gatewaying Between X.400 and Internet Mail*
2. *An Indexer's Guide to the Internet*

3. *An Internet Primer for Information Professionals: A Basic Guide to Internet*
4. *Business User's Guide to the Internet*
5. *E-Mail Companion: Communications Effectively Via the Internet*
6. *Firewalls and Internet Security: Repelling the Wily Hacker*
7. *How to Make a Fortune on the Information Superhighway*
8. *Information Superhighway: Beyond the Internet*
9. *Internet Business Handbook*
10. *Internet Commercial User's Guide*
11. *Internet Connections: A Librarian's Guide to Dial-Up Access and Use*
12. *Internet Handbook for Law Librarians*
13. *Internet Security*
14. *Internet Servers: A Step-by-Step Guide on How to Build Them*
15. *Internet Technology Series, Volume I: Routing*
16. *Internet Technology Series: Domain Name System*
17. *Internet: Domain Administration*
18. *Librarians on the Internet: Impact on Reference Services*
19. *Libraries and the Internet*
20. *Making Money on the Internet*
21. *Managing Internet Information Services: World Wide Web, Gopher, FTP, and More*
22. *Marketing on the Internet: A Step-by-Step Guide for Planning, Promoting Your Business*
23. *Networks 2000: Internet, Information Highway Multimedia Networks, and Beyond*
24. *On Internet 1994: An International Guide to Electronic Journals, Newsletters*
25. *On Internet Ninety-Five: An International Guide to Resources on the Internet*
26. *Promises and Pitfalls: A Briefing Paper on Internet Publishing*
27. *Publishing on the Internet: Mac Edition*
28. *Publishing on the Internet: Windows Edition*
29. *Search Sheets for OPACs on the Internet, 1994*
30. *Success with Internet*
31. *The Internet and Special Librarians: Use, Training, and the Future*
32. *The Internet Hacker's Handbook: Twenty Tips for Secure Data Transmission*

33. *The Internet Library: Case Studies of Library Internet Management and Use*
34. *The Legal List: Law-Related Resources on the Internet and Elsewhere*
35. *The Online Journalist: Using the Internet and Other Electronic Resources*
36. *Troubleshooting TCP-IP: Analyzing the Protocols of the Internet*
37. *WAIS and Gopher Servers: A Guide for Librarians and Internet End-Users*
38. *Way of the Ferret: Finding Educational Resources on the Internet*
39. *Wired for Business: Insider's Guide to Doing Business on the Internet*

10 | Internet Sites for Business Research

This chapter presents an overview of business use of the Internet and gives examples of information sites of commercial value on the Internet. The Internet is important to businesses in many areas such as sales, marketing, public relations, and communication. For secondary marketing research, information is the important issue. The sites mentioned are examples of sites with satisfactory information content, quality, and accessibility. They are only a sample and are chosen to illustrate the range and types of information available.

Business and the Internet: An Uneasy Peace

Business's rapidly increasing presence on the Internet is unsettling to many of the longtime users of the Net—academics, government types, students, and hobbyists. As researchers, we are not the area of controversy. However, the changes affect the quantity and types of business information available on the Internet. In the long run, increased commercialization will make the Internet more useful to us.

There are some simple suggestions to minimize a business's impact:

- Don't send unsolicited E-mail. Multiple mailings of unsolicited E-mail create ill will for your business or marketing research project.

- You should trade information for support. In your E-mail or mail list postings, provide free useful information. Then when you want something, people will help you.

- Home pages on the Web are a useful information-exchange tool. Offer information, pictures, references, or other valuable things and people will come to you and read your marketing information. People will even provide information (such as answering market surveys using forms) when visiting interesting sites or in exchange for free information returned by E-mail.

> There are excellent books discussing business on the Internet. Some are listed in "For Further Reading" at the end of the chapter.

Another issue for business use of the Internet is security—hackers, thieves, mistakes, and other things. This is an important consideration that requires close monitoring, as it strongly influences the real usefulness of the Internet. Secure systems are rapidly being developed.

Web Sites

Where should you go on the Internet? I use the Internet as one of my research tools. So I am always reviewing World Wide Web and other Internet sites for useful and accurate information. The Internet sites listed in this chapter are ones I have found worthwhile. The sites are not guaranteed to be available or to be at the same URL when you read this book (sometimes they change the day after I find them). This rapid change is one of the major problems in using the Internet for research.

> For my latest list of sites, visit my Web page at http://www.vivamus.com.

Company Information

- New Product Announcements—a Usenet archive for new product announcements: http://fohnix.metronet.com:80/newprod/newprod.html
- Commercial Server Directory: http://www.directory.net
- Internet Business Center: http://www.tig.com/IBC/
- Apollo Advertising—free advertising: http://apollo.co.uk/home.html

One of the best sources of individual company information has become home pages placed by those companies on the Net. Companies such as IBM maintain home pages providing easy access to annual reports, product announcements, product catalogs, research and development information, and general company information. This very up-to-date information is an ideal starting point for company and industry studies. Figure 10-1 shows IBM's home page.

Computers and Technology

- Institute of Electrical and Electronic Engineers: http://www.ieee.org
- Tektronix: http://www.tek.com
- Apple Computer: http://www.apple.com
- Welcome to Intel: http://www.intel.com
- Silicon Graphics: http://www.sgi.com
- Hewlett-Packard: http://www.hp.com
- Sun Microsystems: http://www.sun.com
- Digital Equipment Corporation: http://www.dec.com
- IBM: http://www.ibm.com
- Cray Research: http://www.cray.com
- Dell Computer: http://www.dell.com
- Microsoft Corporation: http://www.microsoft.com

Figure 10-1
IBM's home page

Financial Information

- Quote.Com. Stock quotes: http://www.quote.com
- NETworth Information Page: http://networth.galt.com/www/home/networth.htm
- FINWeb Home Page: http://riskweb.bus.utexas.edu:80/finweb.html
- Security APL Quote Server: http://www.secapl.com/cgi-bin/qs
- CTSNET Business and Finance Center: http://CRASH.CTS.COM/cts/biz/
- Dow Jones Industrial Average: http://www.secapl.com/secapl/quoteserver/djia.htm

General Business Information

- Home Business Review: http://www.tab.com/Home.Business/
- Rice Subject Information: http://riceinfo.rice.edu/RiceInfo/Subject.html
- Babson Internet Business Resource Links: gopher://gopher.babson.edu
- Internet Business Center—a useful site with pointers to other useful sites: http://www.tig.com/IBC
- CommerceNet Home: http://www.commerce.net

Government Information

- Commerce Department: http://www.doc.gov
- FedWorld: http://www.fedworld.gov—see Table 10-1 for a list of some available sources
- Statistics—extensive business statistics: http://www.stat-usa.gov
- National Technology Transfer Center—federal technology available for licensing: http://iridium.nttc.edu/nttc.html

Table 10-1   Some U.S. Government Computer Systems You Can Reach from FedWorld

SITE	AGENCY	DATABASE
CIC-BBS	General Services Administration	Consumer Information Center
DMIE	National Institute of Standards and Technology	NIST Data Management Information
EBB	Commerce Department	Economic data and information
ELISA system	Department of Defense	DoD Export License Tracking System
EPUB	Department of Energy	Energy information and data
FDA's BBS	Food and Drug Administration	Food and Drug Administration info and policies
FERC-CIPS	Department of Energy	Federal Energy Regulatory Commission
IM/EXBANK	Department of Commerce	Import/Export Bank data and info
LABOR NEWS	Department of Labor	Department of Labor information and files
MEGAWATT 1	Department of Energy	Information on Energy and DoE
OERI	Department of Education	Educational research and improvement
SBA ON LINE	Small Business Administration	SBA information and data (9600 bps)
TELENEWS	Department of Energy	Data and info on fossil fuels
USCS BBS	Customs	Customs and exchange rate data & info
USGS BBS	United States Information Agency	Geological Survey BBS/CD-ROM info
OASH BBS	Department of Health and Human Services	Health & AIDS information & reports
GPSIC	United States Coast Guard	GPS, Loran & Omega info
LC NEWS SERV	Library of Congress	Library of Congress News Service
STIS	National Science Foundation	Science & Technology Info System
NOAA-ESDD	National Oceanic and Atmospheric Administration	NOAA Earth System Data Directory
PIM BBS	Environmental Protection Agency	Pesticide Information Network
CABB	State Department	Passport information/travel alerts
FCC-STATE LINK	Federal Communications Commission	FCC Daily Digest & Carrier Stats/Report
HUD-N&E BBS	Department of Housing and Urban Development	HUD News & Events BBS/press releases

(continued)

Table 10-1   *(continued)*

SITE	AGENCY	DATABASE
FREND	National Archives	Federal Register Electronic News Delivery
IRS-SOI	Internal Revenue Service	Public taxpayer statistical information
BHP BBS	Department of Health and Human Services	Medical & health services information
MARINE DATA	National Oceanic and Atmospheric Administration	Marine databases & files
CALL-ERS BBS	United States Department of Agriculture	Agriculture Economic Research Service

International Information

- U.S.–Japan Technology Management Center—our starting point for Japanese research: http://fuji.stanford.edu
- Ken Lunde's Home Page—Japanese information processing: http://jasper.ora.com/lunde/
- USA-Russia Friends and Partners Project: http://april.ibpm.serpukhov.su:80/friends
- Window to Russia—Russian security market data, Institutional Investors Guide: http://www.kiae.su/www/wtr/
- NTT Home Page—Japan: http://www.ntt.jp
- Asia-Pacific Info Sources: http://emailhost.ait.ac.th/Asia/ asia.html
- Australian Web servers: http://www.csu.edu.au
- European Home Page: http://s700.uminho.pt/europa.html
- European Country Maps: http://www.tue.nl/maps.html

Internet Information

- Welcome to Netscape: http://home.mcom.com
- The InterNIC InfoGuide Home Page: http://www.internic.net/

- HTML FAQ:
  http://www.umcc.umich.edu/~ec/www/ html_faq.html
- A Beginner's Guide to HTML: http://www.ncsa.uiuc.edu/
  General/Internet/WWW/HTMLPrimer.html
- HTML Working and Background Materials:
  http://info.cern.ch/hypertext/WWW/MarkUp/
  MarkUp.html
- Guide to Cyberspace 6.1—Contents:
  http://www.eit.com:80/web/www.guide/
- Guide to Network Resource Tools—Gopher:
  http://www.earn.net/gnrt/gopher.html
- Guide to Network Resource Tools—ARCHIE:
  http://www.earn.net/gnrt/archie.html
- Net Happenings (Indiana University Local Archive):
  http://www-iub.indiana.edu/cgi-bin/nethaps/
- Frequently Asked Questions on WWW:
  http://info.cern.ch/hypertext/WWW/FAQ/List.html
- What is the difference between WAIS, Gopher, and
  WWW?: http://info.cern.ch/hypertext/WWW/FAQ/
  WAISandGopher.html
- World Wide Web FAQ:
  http://sunsite.unc.edu/boutell/faq/www_faq.html

Legal and Intellectual Property Information

- Copyright Clearance Center:
  http://www.directory.net/ copyright/
- STO's Internet Patent Search System:
  http://sunsite.unc.edu/patents/intropat.html
- Net-Lawyers—discussions on lawyers in the online world:
  http://www.webcom.com/~lewrose/home.html
- Coalition for Networked Information—cyberspace-related
  legal issues: gopher://gopher.cni.org

- Cornell Law School: http://www.law.cornell.edu/
- ILTweb RightsBase: http://www.ilt.columbia.edu/gen/ref/ ILTcopy.html
- The NII Intellectual Property Report—analysis of digital copyright issues by Professor Samuelson: http://gnn.com:80/meta/imedia/features/copyright/ samuelson.html
- Questel/Orbit—Patent and Trademark Welcome Page: http://www.questel.orbit.com/patents/
- WWW Virtual Library—Law. Many good links to other sources: http://www.law.indiana.edu/

Leisure and Miscellaneous

- Internet Movie Database Browser: http://www.msstate.edu/Movies/moviequery.html
- World Wide Web servers—Massachusetts: http://sturtevant.com/wwwlist/mas.html
- Mosaic In A Box Home Page: http://www.spry.com/ mbox/index.html
- Home of the Internet Wizard: http://wizard.spry.com/ index.html
- The Sporting Green: http://www.cs.cmu.edu:8001/afs/ cs.cmu.edu/user/landay/pub/www/sports/sports.html
- Ultimate TV List: http://www.tvnet.com/

Libraries, Books, Documents, and Magazines

- Time magazine: http://www.timeinc.com/time/universe.html
- Electronic Newsstand—business publications and resources and travel publications: http://www.enews.com/
- Ziff-Davis Publishing Company: http://www.ziff.com

- University of Houston: http://info.lib.uh.edu
- Yale University: gopher://yaleinfo.yale.edu
- HotWired—Wired magazine: http://www.hotwired.com
- Hype ElectraZine: http://www.phantom.com/~giant/ hype.html

News

- TimesFax—Internet version of the *New York Times* (requires Adobe Acrobat reader—available free): http://nytimesfax.com
- Voice of America News Wire: gopher://ftp.voa.gov/11/ newswire
- Interactive Weather Browser: http://rs560.cl.msu.edu/ weather/interactive.html
- Mercury Center Web: http://www.sjmercury.com

Information Sources

- DIALOG Home Page: http://www.dialog.com
- CompuServe Home Page: http://www.compuserve.com
- LEXIS-NEXIS Communication Center: http://www.lexis-nexis.com

Science

- NASA Information Services: http://hypatia.gsfc.nasa.gov/ NASA_homepage.html
- Listing of Researchers and Sites: http://www.gatech.edu/ techhome/Research.html
- University of California Museum of Paleontology: http://ucmp1.berkeley.edu/

- ArchNet—University of Connecticut Anthropology Department: http://spirit.lib.uconn.edu/ArchNet/ArchNet.html
- Space Shuttle Challenger Accident: http://rossi.astro.nwu.edu/lentz/space/feynman-report.html
- Closing of the Endless Frontier: http://string.harvard.edu/ docs/feynman.html
- Overview of Nanotechnology: http://planchet.rutgers.edu/ intro.html
- The Nine Planets: http://seds.lpl.arizona.edu/ nineplanets/nineplanets/nineplanets.html

Search Tools for the Internet

This rapidly growing (and still immature) area is very important for the business and market researcher. Two Web sites I have recently begun using are discussed here along with a URL list of other sites for search tools.

In May 1995 the Library Corporation introduced the NlightN online information service at http://www.nlightn.com. Pricing is transaction-based. The NlightN Division of the Library Corporation is based at 1807 Michael Faraday Court, Reston, VA (800-654-4486).

The site features the world's largest single index, the NlightN Universal Index, which allows users to locate data stored in more than 500 public and private databases, news services, and the Internet. (NlightN is aggressively pursuing more data sources.) Users enter a word or phrase and the location of applicable information is returned. Information stored in electronic form can be delivered online. Other material, such as books, maps, dissertations, and articles not stored electronically may be ordered and delivered by fax, mail, or overnight delivery.

NlightN currently offers access to a wide variety of sources, including the Library of Congress, National Library of Medicine, British Library, Cambridge Scientific Abstracts, ABI/INFORM, SPORT Database, Merriam-Webster, Film Literature Index, Magazine Articles Summary, Reader's Guide to Periodic Literature, US Patents, Dissertation Abstracts, various newswires, World Wide Web sites, and many others. The Lycos search tool is integrated into the NlightN service.

The All-in-One Search Page located at http://www.albany.net/~wcross/all1srch.html is a compilation of various forms-based search tools found on the Internet. It is created by William Cross. They have been combined here to form a consistent interface and convenient all-in-one search point. This site provides search tools for the World Wide Web, the General Internet, Software, People, News, Publications, Technical Reports, Documentation, Desk Reference, and Other Searches/Services.

- InfoSeek Home Page: http://www.infoseek.com:80/Home
- WWW Virtual Library—a good place to start searching: http://www.w3.org/hypertext/DataSources/bySubject
- W3 Search Engines: http://web.nexor.co.uk/susi/cusi.html
- WWWW—the WORLD WIDE WEB WORM: http://www.cs.colorado.edu/home/mcbryan/WWWW.html
- The Whole Internet Catalog: http://nearnet.gnn.com/gnn/wic/index.html
- The Lycos Home Page—Hunting WWW Information: http://lycos.cs.cmu.edu/
- Yahoo: http://www.yahoo.com
- WebCrawler Home Page: http://webcrawler.cs.washington.edu/WebCrawler/Home.html
- NIKOS Gateway: http://www.rns.com/cgi-bin/nikos
- Harvest: http://harvest.cs.colorado.edu
- More W3 Search Engines: http://cuiwww.unige.ch/meta-index.html

- MS160 ARCHIE Server Gateway:
  http://www.pvv.unit.no/archie
- PLWebServer: http://www.pls.com

Ask the Experts

One powerful secondary marketing research use of the Internet is locating and contacting experts. In addition, you may frequently find help just by asking. To get help, try doing the following:

- Search the lists of Usenet FAQs to see if one covers your topic.
- If there isn't an FAQ, search the list of Usenet forums, to find an appropriate forum for your question.
- Then search the LISTSERV lists to find an appropriate group for your question.

If you want to locate a specific individual on the Internet, start with the telephone and just ask for the Net address. If that is not possible, some crude tools are available. WHO'S ONLINE is an experimental "hyperbiographical" database; people place their own information online. (It is found at http://www.ictp.trieste.it/Canessa/ENTRIES/entries.html.) FINGER is a personal Yellow Pages system available on some sites; check at the site you are interested in.

A good reference for looking for experts is provided at the end of this chapter.

Summary

So—what's the problem? There is an immense amount of information on the Internet. Why then is it not perfect for the secondary marketing researcher? There are several reasons:

- Although search tools are improving, it is still both difficult and slow to find the exact information desired.
- Much information is not available yet:
  - —Archival records more than a few years old
  - —Private company information
  - —International company information
  - —Information about subsidiaries of major companies
  - —Company directories
  - —Business and trade association information
- Data quality, reliability, and accessibility remain important issues. Many Internet resources are established by volunteer or nonprofit organizations. This reduces cost but also reduces the incentive to maintain the highest quality. For example, I once discovered what seemed to be the perfect resource for a research project only to find that the graduate student who was developing it quit (or graduated) halfway through.
- Time and effort are required to develop and maintain search skills and to keep track of the rapid changes.

For Further Reading

1. *The Internet Yellow Pages,* by Harley Hahn and Rick Stout (Osborne McGraw-Hill, 1994). Generally considered to be one of the best site listing books.
2. *The Internet Directory,* by Eric Braun (Fawcett Columbine, 1994). Another good book of sites.
3. Internet business books—there are several books written about business and the Internet that I have found useful:
   - *The Internet Business Companion,* by David Angell and Brent Heslop (Addison-Wesley, 1995). Very readable introduction to the Internet and business applications.

- *The Internet Business Book*, by Jill Ellsworth and Matthew Ellsworth (Wiley, 1994).
- *The Internet Business Guide*, by Rosiland Resnick and Dave Taylor (SAMS, 1994).
- *Doing Business on the Internet*, by Mary J. Cronin (Van Nostrand Reinhold, 1994). My favorite of these books.

4. *Internet Business Advantage* is a monthly newsletter from Wentworth WorldWide Media, Inc., that provides very good articles on Internet business happenings—great for keeping up with new, useful sites.

5. *Gale Guide to Internet Databases*, edited by Joanne Zakalik (Gale Research, Inc., 1995). Contact Gale Research, Inc., P.O. Box 33477, Detroit, MI 48232-5477; 800-877-4253. A new publication providing information on 2000 Internet information sites. Although like all Internet site guides, it is already out of date, it is a very useful book. The book is well indexed (by host, format, name, and subject) and has a valuable Internet glossary and bibliography.

6. The Library of Congress Information System (LOCIS) *Reference Manual* and *Quick Search Guide* are valuable tools for accessing and using the Library of Congress. These two inexpensive manuals, available from the Library of Congress, provide instructions with examples for online searching of the LOC. If you plan to make significant use of this valuable source of information, you should buy these books. They are available online at ftp.loc.gov/pub/lc.online.

7. "Tracking Down Experts with Online Resources," by John E. Schumacher and Donna R. Dolan, *Database* (June–July 1995): p. 14.

11 | *Using the World Wide Web and the Internet for Secondary Marketing Research*

This chapter offers specific examples of searches for secondary marketing research information on the Internet and the World Wide Web. The chapter reviews search tools, Web browsers, Web search tools, and sample projects.

> Search tools for the Internet and, particularly, the World Wide Web, is a "hot" area. I expect a great deal of progress, with new for-fee tools appearing rapidly. Please watch my Web site (http://www.vivamus.com) for the latest list of Web search tools.

Searching the Old Internet—Before the Web

In the previous chapters we have looked at the Internet and Internet tools. We have discussed FTP, Telnet, Gopher, ARCHIE, VERONICA, and WAIS. Searching the Internet used to require using a UNIX shell program together with those tools. The Internet was a purely text-based interface, not known for ease of use. Skill, time, and patience were required to perform any kind of research. Until recently, I did not find the Internet particularly useful for secondary market research—only limited information could be found while the client was screaming for results yesterday. Now, with the rapid growth of the Internet and the World Wide Web, the situation is changing. In 1995 I finally find the Internet to be one of the tools necessary for the professional researcher to provide the best value to clients. The Internet, particularly the World Wide Web, still has a long way to go, but it is much improved.

UnCover, the Library of Congress, and Census data are examples of currently useful Internet information sites. They will be briefly illustrated next.

UnCover (called the article access and delivery solution) contains records describing journals and their contents. It is an online table of contents for more than 16,000 magazines and journals. More than 5000 current citations are added daily. Searching the database is *free*—you pay only for articles ordered. UnCover has online help, and a user's guide is available. Call 800-221-3306.

> Access UnCover by Telnet to database.carl.org or via the Web at
> http://www.carl.org/uncover/unchome.html

UnCover offers you the opportunity to order fax copies of articles from the database. To order an article from the UnCover database, perform a search to locate the article you want and then mark the article. Once you have marked all of the articles you wish to order, order the articles by following the on-screen directions. Articles will be delivered directly to your fax machine in as fast as twenty-four hours. Costs for delivery (including copyright fees) are displayed on-screen and can be paid by credit card or deposit account.

UnCover Reveal is a new addition—an electronic-mail alert service. This low-cost service allows users to monitor up to fifty journals and receive the tables of contents automatically. Search strategies may also be performed weekly, with the results sent by E-mail. Call 800-221-3306.

The Library of Congress is a valuable research resource: for example, one can access copyrights there. The Library of Congress is available through Fedworld (http://www.fedworld.gov), via Telnet to locis.loc.gov, via Gopher to marvel.loc.gov, and via the Web at http://lcweb.loc.gov/homepage/lchp.html. A marvelous resource, it requires some effort to use efficiently—and like any great library, it is a splendid way to waste time.

Another valuable Internet site is direct access to the Census. Census information can be reached via Fedworld, the Department of Commerce (http://www.doc.gov), or directly at http://www.census.gov. Figure 11-1 shows the Census home page.

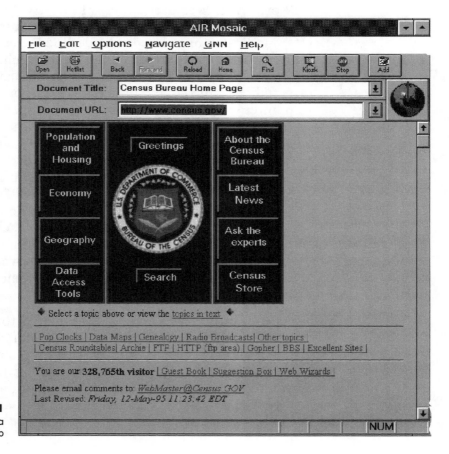

Figure 11-1
Get Census information via the World Wide Web

Browsers—Viewing the Web

Web browsers were discussed briefly in Chapter 5. They are evolving rapidly, becoming better and cheaper. Every day a new browser or an update of an existing one appears with more features and better performance.

When you first open a browser, it connects to the Internet through a TCP/IP interface. It loads the default home page you have set in your configuration (look at Figure 11-1 for reference). To move to other resources on the Internet, the World Wide Web uses hyperlinks (also called anchors or hot spots) to allow you to jump to other resources. Hyperlinks are indicated by colored or underlined text, or by graphics surrounded by a colored border (you can change the color that is used). Another way to tell that you are on a hyperlink is to highlight the text or graphic with your mouse; the pointer will appear as a hand. You can then click on a hyperlink to connect to another Mosaic document. As you become an experienced browser, you'll be able to build a library of home pages that you like, using a "hotlist" or bookmarks. You can also travel through Mosaic documents you encounter using the buttons for Back and Forward or the pull-down lists: Document Title, Document URL, or History. For example, you can click on the Back button to move back to the last document you viewed. The Forward button can move you forward after you have moved back. You can also type B for Back or F for Forward, or choose Back or Forward from the Navigate menu.

At any time, you can click the Home button on the Toolbar, or choose Home from the Navigate menu to return to the document defined as your home page. You can reload the current document at any time by clicking the Reload button; you might want to do this if a document did not load properly. You can also cancel the current task at any time by clicking the Stop button.

One of a browser's most valuable features is its ability to organize the information that you find on the World Wide Web. There are so many documents out there that some form of easy organization is extremely valuable. AIR Mosaic, for example, provides an easy way to organize documents by using hotlists; other browsers may offer a similar feature. It is valuable to be able to group resource locations by subject or by any other criteria. Most browsers come with a pre-loaded set of resource locations, and it is very easy to add locations to the set.

Another feature common to browsers is a status bar—on AIR Mosaic, it is at the bottom. The status bar provides information on the communications in progress. For example, it may tell you that you have downloaded 12,674 bytes of 30,000 bytes.

One problem with the Internet is speed. Communications can seem agonizingly slow over any modem. Graphics take the longest, so a useful feature for a browser is to be able to skip graphics. Many home pages have a text-only version in order to achieve the same result. Another useful feature, common in the latest browsers, is the ability to display all the text before all the graphics are transmitted.

Searching the New Internet—Web Tools

For our purpose, the most important Internet news is the continued development of search tools for the World Wide Web. Existing tools have improved and new tools have appeared. For purposes of demonstration, we will look briefly at the World Wide Web Worm, an older search engine. A newer system called InfoSeek will be used for our test search. With commercial backing, more stable and powerful search tools are becoming available for the Web. However, these new search tools are still evolving.

World Wide Web Worm

The World Wide Web Worm (WWWW) is a World Wide Web search engine that you can use to search for information of interest worldwide. WWWW is located at http://www.cs.colorado.edu/home/mcbryan/WWWW.html. See Figure 11-2 for the WWWW access page.

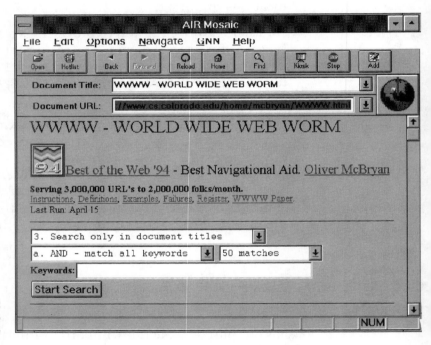

Figure 11-2
Use the World Wide Web Worm to find things

WWWW allows you to locate almost any Web hypertext or information resource (URL) simply by specifying some keywords. Four types of databases are available for searching:

1. Search all URL references.

2. Search all URL addresses.

3. Search all document titles.

4. Search all document addresses.

You can search using AND or OR logic and you can specify the maximum number of documents to be retrieved. Default selections are shown in Figure 11-2.

Note that WWWW is case insensitive and it lets you specify a limit for the number of matches. For these searches, keywords must be at least three characters long and consist of only letters and digits. I tested its search capability: it must be OK—it found my home page.

InfoSeek— A New Commercial Search Tool

According to the vendor, InfoSeek makes searching for information fast, easy, and fun. You can enter a query in plain English or enter just key words and phrases. In response, you get back a list of the article titles that are most relevant to your query. Click on a title and the full text of that article is returned. Figure 11-3 shows the InfoSeek interface.

InfoSeek plans to be convenient one-stop shopping for a variety of both public and commercial data sources. Look for product reviews, phone numbers, or a list of Clint Eastwood's movies here. InfoSeek includes

- An index of WWW pages
- An index of Usenet news (more than 10,000 newsgroups)
- Full-text contents of more than fifty newspapers and magazines about computers
- Newswires from Reuters, Associated Press, Businesswire, PR Newswire, and the Newsbytes News Network
- Detailed company profiles
- Movie reviews, book reviews, and video reviews

Result pages repeat the question, show what words in the query statement were not used in the search, and list databases selected.

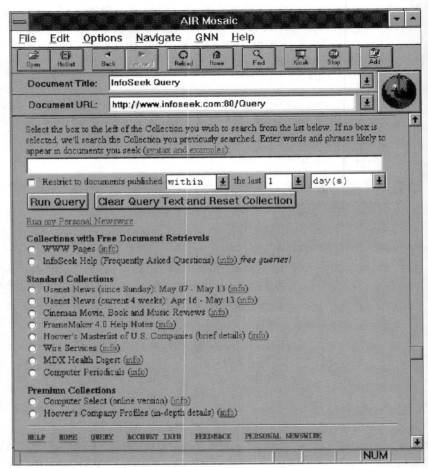

Figure 11-3
InfoSeek has an
easy-to-use interface

Titles of documents found are listed twenty at a time. Each citation names the document, its source, publication (posting) date, and size. A number in square brackets is a relative score of the relevance of the document to our query. Each document title is a hypertext link to the document.

Retrieve a document for review by clicking on it. In the retrieved documents, key words in the search query are highlighted in the text. For long articles, the search software scrolls to the first appearance of the search term(s).

The Test Case

"We're thinking of selling a new product putting Global Positioning System (GPS) receivers in taxis so that taxi companies can track drivers and drivers can find locations. What can you tell me about this?"

The test case was run using professional services in Chapter 8 and will also be run using consumer databases in Chapter 14.

Define and Understand the Problem

As defined in Chapter 8, the information needed (besides the patent search, which won't be repeated) is limited to the following:

1. Recent industry news. What's been written in papers and magazines?
2. A brief company overview of a major GPS manufacturer—Trimble Navigation.

Understand the Vocabulary of Your Problem

The key words and phrases for search terms are specified as *GPS* or *Global Positioning System; taxis* or *taxicabs; navigate* or *navigation* or *navigating* or *locate* or *location* or *locating;* and *track* or *tracking.* The news search is limited to this year and last year.

Determine Appropriate Sources

The choice of sources is not obvious yet on the Internet. On InfoSeek for this example, I will use the WWW pages index, the Usenet News index, and company profiles. The sources can only be used one at a time, and the searches are always full-text.

Create the Research Strategy

The research strategy will use the InfoSeek rules:

- Type your question in plain English using proper capitalization if desired—words and phrases are also permitted.
- Put a comma between unrelated capitalized proper names.
- Place double quotes (") around words that should be adjacent.
- A hyphen can be used instead of double quotes.
- Put brackets around words that should be near each other in any order.
- Add a plus (+) in front of a required word or phrase.
- Capitalize proper names just as you normally would (people, companies, product names, cities, and so on).
- Truncation is automatic—you always get plurals.

Using the InfoSeek search rules, I searched "[+gps +taxi]."

Go Online

A search of the WWW pages found three titles, of which one, the Sennottby page, was useful.

- The Natural Area Coding (NAC) Home Page
- Dr. James Sennottby Page
- Guide: Index3 . 3D Movies, How To See Them On Your Own TV

Look at Usenet News (current 4 weeks): Apr 16–May 13 found seven titles, of which one was interesting—but more of a request for help than a source of information:

- HELP! TAXI POSITIONING SYSTEM!—[836] sci.geo.satellite-nav, jaisrar@chat.carleton.ca (Junaid Ahmed Israr), Tue, 9 May 1995 14:45:28 GMT

Searching general directory information on InfoSeek for Trimble Navigation Limited led to the Hoover's Masterlist of U.S. Companies (brief details), where information was found.

Summary

In this chapter I have primarily reviewed the use of search tools on the World Wide Web in order to perform secondary marketing research. New and evolving search tools such as InfoSeek and the World Wide Web Worm provide hope that the Internet may be useful in the future.

The search results were encouraging but not complete. Although no charges other than normal communications charges were incurred, the searches took about thirty minutes to complete. Some useful information was found. However, it was much less complete than the information that was obtained (quickly and efficiently) from DIALOG.

A major value of the Internet is finding new search ideas and people's names. For a client who wanted a comprehensive result, I would contact some of the people identified in the InfoSeek results.

12 | *The Consumer Sources—Characteristics*

In this chapter I present a brief introduction to the characteristics of the most familiar part of the online world—the consumer sources such as DELPHI, eWorld, CompuServe, America Online (AOL), and Prodigy. The next chapter provides additional details on CompuServe, America Online, and Prodigy.

An Overview

The most-used online services at home are the consumer sources, such as CompuServe, AOL, and Prodigy. Although not designed as professional information sources, these services offer an ever-increasing amount of valuable information. In addition, they provide access (called gateways) to professional services and to the Internet. The consumer services software is very inexpensive (or free) and frequently arrives preinstalled on newly purchased computers.

The advantages of the consumer sources are these:

- Easy to start up (the software was already installed on my newest computer).
- Relatively low cost.
- Easy access through national networks of local telephone numbers or 800 numbers.
- Friendly, easy-to-use interfaces—graphical and attractive.

- A broad range of information—many consumer-oriented services such as sports, games, travel, new cars, *Consumer Reports,* and reference materials. Many family- and child-oriented services are also available.
- Shopping areas or "electronic malls."
- Stock information and trading.

A very important feature of the consumer sources is the special interest groups (also called forums, mailing lists, roundtables, or SIGs). These areas are grouped by subject. They typically include a message area, where members discuss related topics, and a library area, where software and text files are available.

Most of the consumer services have monthly basic fees, with added charges for extended usage time or for special features and services. The major disadvantages for the professional searcher or market researcher include the following:

- The lack of powerful search tools for fast information access
- Incomplete information

On the consumer sources, current, consumer-oriented information is emphasized. The consumer services are mass-marketed to the at-home end user. As a consequence, they do not emphasize support to professionals.

The Big Three

In the spring of 1995, the three largest and most important consumer services are CompuServe, America Online, and Prodigy. Each claims to be the largest or most popular service.

America Online

America Online is growing rapidly as new services and features are added every day. According to AOL, "AOL is now the most popular online service in the country." The growth rate has been very impressive: from approximately 800,000 members in May 1994 to 2.5 million members in May 1995. AOL was one the first services to offer access to the Internet and now has a very nicely integrated Web browser.

AOL supplies very attractive, easy-to-use software. AOL has an impressive (and growing) list of online newspapers and magazines, such as *Business Week, Time, Chicago Tribune, New York Times*, and *San Jose Mercury-News.* The graphical interfaces to these magazines and newspapers make them very appealing and fun to use. AOL also provides unlimited E-mail usage.

AOL has an interesting approach to integrating the Internet and World Wide Web into the service. A common complaint about the Web is that finding desired information is random and difficult. Each of AOL's fourteen service categories has a related selection of popular Web sites, arranged by topic of interest. For example, the best reference-related Web sites will be found under Reference. On AOL, you can have Web pages and AOL screens open simultaneously.

However, there are some usage problems: the system is always downloading new graphics (which seems to take forever) and sometimes has communications overloads due to the rapid growth.

AOL can be reached at 800-827-3338 or on the Internet at http://www.blue.aol.com.

CompuServe

The CompuServe Information Service has been a major supplier of online information, software, and communications services for the public for more than twenty years. In a May

1995 press release, Maury Cox, CompuServe president and CEO, announced, "After a year of record growth, our online community now includes more than three million members who access CompuServe from around the world. No other online service matches our popularity, our services, or our global community spirit." CompuServe is a truly international service, including personal computer users in more than 150 countries.

CompuServe offers global E-mail, a monthly CD-ROM, libraries of free software, nearly 2500 databases, access at up to 28.8 Kbps, and rapidly increasing Internet services. Access is provided to a Web browser, but as a separate piece of software using the same communications line. You cannot access the Web and the main system at the same time.

When you join CompuServe, the basic monthly fee provides unlimited connect time to 100 basic services. For a $9.95 monthly fee, members have unlimited access to more than 120 services, including daily worldwide news, weather, and sports reports and three free hours of Internet access.

Premium services (known as Extended Services) are available on a pay-as-you-go basis at any time. CompuServe charges extra for database access. With more than fifty databases available, CompuServe is a major information provider. CompuServe's online international newsstand features more than 200 general interest and niche publications, dozens of syndicated columnists, and more than 900 entertainment, hobby, games, and special interest forums. AP OnLine is updated hourly, and more than fifty-five newspapers are archived. Many magazines, such as *People* and *Sports Illustrated,* are available. CompuServe provides a total of more than 3000 services, with a wide variety of business and technical resources.

CompuServe offers the most depth and breadth in the consumer online services industry. With a huge array of offerings ranging from downloadable music to machine-based language translation services, CompuServe has served as a catalyst to get people and companies online. New products such as the award-winning CompuServe NetLauncher World Wide Web browser and the CompuServe Viewer, which combines still video images with closed-captioned text and live chat, make the CompuServe Information Service an even more exciting place for the online consumer.

CompuServe is accessible twenty-four hours a day. It provides excellent customer service, including inexpensive graphical interface software (WINCIM), a semiautomatic navigator program (CSNAV), and an informative monthly magazine.

CompuServe's world headquarters is in Columbus, Ohio. It is an H&R Block company. CompuServe, Inc., has two other major divisions in addition to the CompuServe Information Service. CompuServe's Network Services Division provides electronic mail, frame relay services, wide and local area networking services, and software to major corporations and government agencies worldwide.

CompuServe's new Internet Division (Spry, Inc.) brings easy Internet access. Benefits include access to the Web using Spry's Internet Mosaic software through CompuServe's extensive communications network.

Contact CompuServe at 800-524-3388 or access its Web page at www.compuserve.com.

Prodigy

Prodigy ("America's leading online service," according to its press releases) from the Prodigy Services Company has more than 2 million members, who use the service approximately 700,000 times a day. It enables personal computer users to access

- Current news—Reuters, UPI, and API Online.
- Homework Helper—targeted for children but useful for adults. It accesses thirty-five periodicals and more than 700 reference books.

- Entertainment and education features.
- Investment portfolio management, including securities trading.
- Travel ticketing.
- Shopping.
- Comprehensive sports coverage.
- The Internet, including the World Wide Web. Prodigy's browser acts as just one more service and is very easy to use.

Prodigy charges a single fee for the first five hours and additional charges for more use. Prodigy provides excellent customer service, including a quarterly newsletter. In 1995 Prodigy will release brand-new software for Windows, to be followed by Macintosh and Windows 95 versions. Prodigy offers free upgrades as new features and services become available.

The latest new feature announced (in May 1995), Home Page Creator, is software that subscribers use for creating Web pages in HTML. Prodigy may be contacted at 800-776-3449.

Microsoft and Many Others

There are many other players in the consumer online industry. DELPHI, GEnie, and eWorld (from Apple) are three other services with strong followings (although smaller in number of users than the three largest).

DELPHI offers complete access to the Internet (currently text-only—expansions are expected). It has business areas, including the Business, Self-Employed, Work at Home, and Small-Business Advertising forums. DELPHI allows the inexpensive creation of your own forum. DELPHI can be reached at 800-695-4005.

eWorld, a new service from Apple (launched in 1994), has excellent Macintosh support and a very easy-to-use graphical interface. The service is still suffering growing pains and (as of spring 1995) did not have Windows software. It has access to E-mail, FTP, and Usenet on the Internet, with enhancements expected. eWorld can be reached at 800-775-4556.

GEnie, another relatively small service, has an unwieldy text-based interface and very limited (E-mail only) Internet access. It does have a very good selection of files available and an active small business section. As with other services, upgrades are expected. GEnie can be reached at 800-638-9636.

The biggest changes in the near future are expected to come from the entry of two giant new players:

- AT&T will launch the Interchange Online Network (purchased from Ziff). Its graphical, multitasking interface will run on Windows and Windows 95. It is expected to use subscription pricing (not connect time).

The current beta version has access to many computing resources as well as the *Washington Post* and *Star Tribune*. One announced site to be added, @vantage, will potentially be of great interest to the market researcher. This service will be provided by Gartner Group, Inc., a firm that helps large companies decide what computers and software to buy. Also on this service will be other consultants, including Dataquest, Inc., Digital Information Group, and Individual, Inc. This site will be available for an added fee.

- Microsoft will launch the Microsoft Network (MSN)—a part of Windows 95. The final beta version accesses various forums (called bulletin boards on MSN), news, sports, weather, Internet newsgroups, and software libraries. MSN has announced the signing of at least 160 U.S. and 75 European information providers. It is expected to provide very complete Internet access. One example is that MSN has licensed the Lycos search tool.

The effect of these and other changes will probably be the continued growth in the number of people using online services. In addition, some of the weaker services may disappear. For the marketing researcher or information professional, it will probably mean more data available from more sources and a continued reduction in cost.

Consumer Sources and the Internet

The Internet is available on all of the major consumer sources. Prodigy, CompuServe, and AOL all have complete access with Web browsers. I expect all of the surviving services to provide full access—greatly increasing the number of people using the Internet (already growing fast). These services also have been announcing significant communications upgrades that will speed data transfer.

CompuServe has announced expansion plans to create the world's largest Internet-ready network. CompuServe plans to provide a Global 28.8-Kbps Local Dial Access (at no extra cost) and to add 1-800-ISDN (Integrated Services Digital Network) access. CompuServe will convert all its existing 42,000 dial ports to V.34-compliant 28.8 Kbps local dial access. It also plans to increase the number of network dial ports to more than 85,000—all supporting 28.8 Kbps.

Access the Internet on CompuServe by using GO commands. GO FTP provides FTP access. GO INETPUBLISH, GO INETFORUM, AND GO INETRESOURCES connect to Internet forums. For the Internet Services area, use GO INTERNET. GO TELNET, GO PPP, and GO USENET connect to Telnet, PPP, and Usenets. For Internet World magazine, use GO IWORLD.

ISDN, offering access speeds of up to 64 Kbps using switched services, was expected to be available on CompuServe via an 800 number in June 1995. Local ISDN access was planned for approximately ten cities by the end of August 1995. All ports in the CompuServe Network now support the Internet PPP protocol.

Prodigy has announced that it will supply members with ISDN access to the Internet. Prodigy customers will be able to access the Internet much more quickly through an arrangement with IBM, Prodigy, BellSouth, NYNEX, and Pacific Bell. With IBM's high-performance 7845/ISDN WaveRunner modem, members in and around San Jose, Woodland Hills, California, Boston, and Nashville will be able to connect at speeds up to 64 Kbps. This service will be expanded to other markets.

Summary

If you search infrequently, the consumer sources are useful. You can obtain a great deal of information by using what is available directly or by using the gateways to other services. By using the gateways, short-term access to DIALOG and other professional services is available without paying yearly costs or adding an expensive connection. For longer term access, the gateways are very expensive.

> Chapters 13 and 14 provide details and examples of using the consumer service for research.

13 | The Consumer Sources—Descriptions

This chapter provides detailed descriptions of features and databases available on the three major consumer sources—CompuServe, Prodigy, and AOL. This information gives the marketing researcher the knowledge necessary to locate valuable information on the consumer sources.

CompuServe

Knowledge Index

The most interesting offering from CompuServe for the marketing researcher is the Knowledge Index (KI) service. It provides access to more than 50,000 journals through more than 100 full-text, directory, and bibliographic databases from DIALOG. KI is actually a subset of DIALOG Information Services—a version that contains a smaller number of databases. KI is an ideal tool for learning online searching, with its combination of low cost and high quality.

> Areas or services on CompuServe are quickly accessed by typing GO and the service code. For Knowledge Index, type GO KI. The GO function is also accessed by clicking on the stoplight icon on the graphical interface—WINCIM.

Databases may be searched with commands or through menu options. Often the full-text article is available online. Otherwise, it can be ordered for prompt delivery. This service is amazingly inexpensive (40 cents per minute added charge). It is accessible only during evenings and weekends, limiting its use for the market researcher.

> Please read and observe the database restrictions; KI is for personal use only.

Knowledge Index is divided into sections for ease of use with the menus. Individual databases are accessed through the command system. Extensive database descriptions and help files are available online for no extra charge—download them and create your own reference manual. Here is an example of the menu system. This menu system provides a structured approach to database selection. First a list of the sections is shown:

1. Agriculture and Nutrition
2. Bibliography—Books and Monographs
3. Business Information
4. Chemistry
5. Computers and Electronics
6. Directories and Reference
7. Education
8. Law and Government
9. Medicine, Biosciences, and Drugs
10. News and Current Affairs
11. Popular Information
12. Science and Technology
13. Social Sciences and Humanities

Select section 3 and Business Information displays a list of relevant groups of databases:

1. Business and Financial News
2. Company Information

3. General Business Information

4. Industry Information

5. International Trade

6. Product Listings and Announcements

Finally, enter a category number (in this case, 3—General Business Information) and the list of databases is displayed:

1. ABI/INFORM

2. Economic Literature Index

3. Harvard Business Review

Once a database has been selected, the menu lets you select a search mode:

1. Subject Search

2. Author Search

3. Journal Search

4. Company Name Search

Now you enter the search request. Logical OR, AND, or NOT may be used to separate concepts. For example, a typical search term might be "market? and research? and cost?"

After the search is processed, the system returns the number of articles selected. Then the menu lets you either review the results or modify the search. The search can be modified several ways:

1. Narrow subject search (logical AND)

2. Widen subject search (logical OR)

3. Replace subject concepts

4. Select limits—publication year, for example

5. Select author(s)

6. Select additional journal(s) (logical OR)

Knowledge Index is inexpensive and easy to use—try it! Remember that it is for personal use only.

> Extensive Knowledge Index help files are available for free online: descriptions of databases, commands, menu structure, printing or ordering results, and so on. Download these files before you start.

Databases

The primary research resources available on CompuServe are found in an extensive area called the Reference Library. This section includes databases on demographic information, articles, directories (products, manufacturers, and households), trademark and legal information, government proceedings, government information, statistics, consumer information, and newsletters. Many of these databases are similar to the ones on the professional providers. These databases have added charges beyond the basic monthly CompuServe fee. Help files and detailed descriptions of these files are available online for free. Some of the most interesting business files in the Reference Library are listed here (with GO words):

- **Biz*File (GO BIZFILE).** Access to more than 10 million U.S. and Canadian business establishments. Each business is listed by business (company) name, address, telephone number, and length of time it has been listed in the Yellow Pages. You can search the database by company name, geographical location, telephone number, or type of business. Available twenty-four hours a day.

- **Business Database Plus (GO BUSDB).** Search for and retrieve full-text articles from more than 500 regional, national, and international business and trade publications. BDP gives you seven methods to locate articles that can provide you with sales and marketing ideas, product news, industry trends, and analysis.

- **Business Demographics (GO BUSDEM).** Reports designed to help businesses analyze their markets. Two types of reports are available: The Business to Business Report details all major business categories (as represented by SIC codes) by number of employees. The Advertisers Service Report provides employee counts and number of establishments by employee size for retail trade businesses.

- **CENDATA, The Census Bureau Service (GO CENDATA).** The Census Bureau offers tabular data and reports on manufacturing, housing starts, population, agriculture, and more. CENDATA also has the latest press releases from the Census Bureau.

- **Computer Database Plus (GO COMPDB).** A comprehensive collection of computer-related data. Includes about 200 journals, including *PC Magazine, Byte, Digital Review, MacUser, PC Week,* and *PC World* dating from 1987. More than 370,000 articles. Search by subject, company name, product name, featured people, publication name, and date. Updated weekly.

- **Computer Directory (GO COMPDIR).** Provides information on more than 74,000 hardware, software, peripheral, data communications, and telecommunications products and more than 13,000 manufacturers. Information includes the manufacturer's name, key specifications, compatibility information, and pricing data. Company listings provide directory information.

- **Data-Processing Newsletters (GO DPNEWS).** Full text of articles taken from several of the leading newsletters covering the computer, electronics, and telecommunications industries.

- **Demographics (GO DEMOGRAPHICS).** Demographic information for any area of the United States. Information includes the population as well as the income, age, and race of the residents. The data is based on the 1990 Census and current year and five-year forecasts.

- **Government Information (GO GOVERNMENT).** A menu of information on government services and publications.

- **Government Publications (GO GPO).** The first part is a catalog of government publications, books, and subscription services that may be ordered online from the Government Printing Office. The second part is online consumer information articles from government publications.

- **Legal Research Center (GO LEGALRC).** Access to seven databases containing indexes to articles from more than 750 law journals, publications, studies, and other sources covering practical and theoretical aspects of criminal justice, criminology, and law enforcement. It includes summaries of documents covering federal taxation, banking, and finance.

- **Magazine Database Plus (GO MAGDB).** Full-text magazine articles from more than ninety publications.

- **Marketing/Management Research (GO MGMTRC).** Offers access to nine databases (ABI/INFORM, Findex, FINIS, Industry Data Sources, Infomat International Business, McGraw-Hill Publications Online, PTS MARS, PTS New Product Announcements, and PTS PROMT). It contains major U.S. and international business, management, and technical magazines; market and industry research reports, market studies, and statistical reports; and U.S. and international company news releases.

- **Marquis Who's Who (GO BIOGRAPHY).** Provides biographical information on key North American professionals.

- **Neighborhood Report (GO NEIGHBORHOOD).** Demographic makeup of any ZIP code in the United States. Population, race, and age breakdowns are displayed on the report, as well as the household income distribution, the types of households, and the occupations of the residents of the neighborhood. Housing patterns for the neighborhood are also examined, including the status of occupied housing, average home value and rent, and the age of housing structures.

- **NTIS—Government Sponsored Research (GO NTIS).** The National Technical Information Service database references government-sponsored research, development, and engineering reports. The database includes information from 1970 to the present.

- **PaperChase (GO PCH).** Access to MEDLINE, the National Library of Medicine's database of references to biomedical literature.

- **Patent Research Center (GO PATENT).** Access to databases containing summaries of U.S. and international patents. Databases include Claims/U.S. Patent Abstracts (1950 to present) and the World Patents Index (1963 to present).

- **Phone*File (GO PHONEFILE).** Contains the names, addresses, and phone numbers of more than 75 million U.S. households.

- **Trademark Research Center (GO TRADERC).** Access to databases containing nongraphic trademarks (for the fifty U.S. states, Puerto Rico, and the federal government). An entry contains the U.S. class, the international class, a description of the service or product, the status of the trademark, the registration date, and the date of first use.

- **UK Marketing (GO UKMARKETING).** Databases contain market research reports compiled by top marketing analysts (primarily on U.K. and international companies). The information is gathered from a variety of sources and includes reports from the ICC Key Note series, Management and Marketing Abstracts, Marketing Surveys Index, Mintel Research Reports and Mintel Special Reports, and MSI Market Research Reports.

IQuest (GO IQUEST) is another major research service on CompuServe. It is a gateway to more than 450 professional databases provided by CD PLUS Technologies, DataStar, DIALOG, FT Profile, NewsNet, Orbit Online Products, Questel, Waterlow Company Services, and the H. W. Wilson Company. IQuest includes historical data, bibliographic, and full-text files. Online real-time help is available in IQuest by typing SOS. The database gateway is a very expensive way to search.

IQuest offers three simple menu-driven ways to retrieve information:

- IQuest-I will choose the appropriate database after a topic is selected. IQuest-I starts with broad subject definitions, narrowing the topic until a single database is recommended. When you select IQuest-I, a menu lists nine broad subject areas: Business; Science and Technology; Medicine and Allied Health; Law and Patents and Trademarks and Brand Names and Copyrights; Social Sciences and Education; Arts and Literature and Religion; Entertainment and Travel; and People and News.

- IQuest-II allows the selection of a specific database. (You should have already used SOS, the database directory, or a prior IQuest-I session to identify the name of the database.) If you misspell the database name, you get a menu listing databases that are alphabetically close to the name that you enter.

- SmartSCAN searches multiple databases. SmartSCAN moves through a series of menus (like IQuest-I) to select the appropriate scan for your topic area.

Another useful feature is IQuest's Database Directory. To obtain detailed information on all of the databases for a given subject area, enter DIR followed by a subject category (for example: DIR FINANCE) at an arrow prompt. IQuest will display descriptions and pricing information for each database relevant to that area.

IQuest is provided to CompuServe by Telebase. A list of all the Telebase services with GO commands appears in Table 13-1. All of these databases cost extra and are expensive.

BiblioData provides a very valuable search aid for CompuServe called *CompuServe Companion: Finding Newspapers and Magazines Online*. This handy book offers detailed information on all full-text databases on CompuServe, including those covered in IQuest and all other Telebase services. Figure 13-1 shows a sample page.

Table 13-1
Access Codes for Some
Interesting Business Data-
bases on CompuServe

Telebase Service	GO Command
Business Dateline	GO BUSDATE
Corporate Affiliations	GO AFFILIATIONS
D&B—Canadian Dun's Market Identifiers	GO DBCAN
D&B—Dun's Electronic Business Directory	GO DUNSEBD
D&B—Dun's Market Identifiers	GO DMI
D&B—International Dun's Market Identifiers	GO DBINT
European Company Research Center	GO EUROLIB
German Company Research Centre	GO GERLIB
Investext	GO INVTEXT
National Technical Information Service	GO NTIS
News Source USA	GO NEWSUSA
Thomas Register Online	GO THOMAS
TRADEMARKSCAN	GO TRD
TRW Business Profiles	GO TRWREPORT
UK Company Research Centre	GO UKLIB
UK Newspaper Library	GO UKPAPERS

Prodigy

Prodigy has a new special feature called Homework Helper.
Though targeted at students, it is easy to use and quite powerful. Homework Helper uses software to connect using the
Prodigy communications link. The Homework Helper service runs on Infonautics' Electronic Printing Press and is
supported by the Commonwealth of Pennsylvania's Ben

Market Europe (Continued)
▲ GO IQUEST: 1294 (PTS PROMT) +++   08/90 - Pres.
GO IQUEST: 2506 (PTS NEWSLETTER DB) +++   08/90 - Pres.
▲ GO MRK: PTS PROMT   08/90 - Pres.

Market Latin America
▲ GO IQUEST: 1294 (PTS PROMT) +++   10/93 - Pres.
GO IQUEST: 2506 (PTS NEWSLETTER DB) +++   10/93 - Pres.
▲ GO MRK: PTS PROMT   10/93 - Pres.

Market Research Europe
▲ GO BUSDB: BUSINESS & TRADE JOURNALS   01/90 - Pres.
▲ GO IQUEST: 1615 (TRADE & INDUST. ASAP) ++ 01/90 - Pres.

Marketing (United Kingdom)
▲ GO BUSDB: BUSINESS & TRADE JOURNALS   01/90 - Pres.
▲ GO IQUEST: 1243 (ABI/INFORM) ++   01/92 - Pres.
▲ GO IQUEST: 1615 (TRADE & INDUST. ASAP) ++ 01/90 - Pres.
GO IQUEST: 2204 ++   Fixed Span
  Freq: Weekly; Span: 12 mon
GO IQUEST: 3133 (TEXTLINE GLOBAL NEWS)   05/83 - Pres.
  Freq: Weekly; Lag: 5 day
▲ GO KI: BUSI1 (ABI/INFORM)   01/92 - Pres.
▲ GO MRK: ABI/INFORM   01/92 - Pres.

Marketing & Media Decisions
See "Mediaweek" which replaces this publication in 1991.
▲ GO BUSDB: BUSINESS & TRADE JOURNALS   05/89 - 01/91
  Span: 5 yr
▲ GO IQUEST: 1615 (TRADE & INDUST. ASAP) ++ 01/83 - 01/91

Marketing Computers
This is an Adweek publication.
▲ GO BUSDB: BUSINESS & TRADE JOURNALS   Fixed Span
  Span: 5 yr
GO IQUEST: 1294 (PTS PROMT) +++   06/90 - Pres.
▲ GO IQUEST: 1615 (TRADE & INDUST. ASAP) ++ 01/89 - Pres.
GO MRK: PTS PROMT   06/90 - Pres.

Marketing Intelligence & Planning
▲ GO IQUEST: 1243 (ABI/INFORM) ++   07/92 - Pres.
▲ GO KI: BUSI1 (ABI/INFORM)   07/92 - Pres.
▲ GO MRK: ABI/INFORM   07/92 - Pres.

Marketing Management
▲ GO IQUEST: 1243 (ABI/INFORM) ++   01/93 - Pres.
▲ GO KI: BUSI1 (ABI/INFORM)   01/93 - Pres.
▲ GO MRK: ABI/INFORM   01/93 - Pres.

Marketing News
▲ GO BUSDB: BUSINESS & TRADE JOURNALS   Fixed Span
  Span: 5 yr
▲ GO IQUEST: 1243 (ABI/INFORM) ++   01/91 - Pres.
▲ GO IQUEST: 1615 (TRADE & INDUST. ASAP) ++ 01/89 - Pres.
▲ GO KI: BUSI1 (ABI/INFORM)   01/91 - Pres.
▲ GO MRK: ABI/INFORM   01/91 - Pres.

Marketing Research
▲ GO IQUEST: 1243 (ABI/INFORM) ++   01/92 - Pres.
▲ GO KI: BUSI1 (ABI/INFORM)   01/92 - Pres.
▲ GO MRK: ABI/INFORM   01/92 - Pres.

Marketing Research Review
GO BUSDB: INDUSTRY NEWSLETTERS   Fixed Span
  Span: 12 mon
▲ GO IQUEST: 1294 (PTS PROMT) +++   10/91 - Pres.
GO IQUEST: 2506 (PTS NEWSLETTER DB) +++   10/91 - Pres.
▲ GO MRK: PTS PROMT   10/91 - Pres.

Marketing to Women
GO BUSDB: INDUSTRY NEWSLETTERS   Fixed Span
  Span: 12 mon
▲ GO IQUEST: 1294 (PTS PROMT) +++   01/91 - Pres.
▲ GO IQUEST: 1762 (PTS MARS) +++   01/91 - Pres.
GO IQUEST: 2506 (PTS NEWSLETTER DB) +++   01/91 - Pres.
▲ GO MRK: PTS MARS   01/91 - Pres.
▲ GO MRK: PTS PROMT   01/91 - Pres.

Marketing Week (United Kingdom)
GO IQUEST: 3133 (TEXTLINE GLOBAL NEWS)   05/83 - Pres.
  Freq: Weekly; Lag: 5 day

Marketletter (United Kingdom)
Available online before the printed publication is out.
GO BUSDB: INDUSTRY NEWSLETTERS   Fixed Span
  Span: 12 mon
▲ GO IQUEST: 1294 (PTS PROMT) +++   01/92 - Pres.
GO IQUEST: 2506 (PTS NEWSLETTER DB) +++   01/92 - Pres.
GO IQUEST: 2844 +   1985 - Pres.
  Freq: Daily; Lag: None
▲ GO MRK: PTS PROMT   01/92 - Pres.

Marshfield News-Herald (Wisconsin)
▲ GO BDL   12/91 - Pres.
▲ GO IQUEST: 2053 (BUSINESS DATELINE) +++ 12/91 - Pres.

Maryland Business & Living
Newspaper from Baltimore, Maryland.
▲ GO BDL   01/85 - 09/85
▲ GO IQUEST: 2053 (BUSINESS DATELINE) +++ 01/85 - 09/85

Mass High Tech (Massachusetts)
▲ GO BDL   09/89 - Pres.
▲ GO IQUEST: 2053 (BUSINESS DATELINE) +++ 09/89 - Pres.

Mass Transit
▲ GO IQUEST: 1615 (TRADE & INDUST. ASAP) ++ 01/91 - Pres.

Massachusetts CPA Review
▲ GO IQUEST: 1243 (ABI/INFORM) ++   01/91 - Pres.
▲ GO KI: BUSI1 (ABI/INFORM)   01/91 - Pres.
▲ GO MRK: ABI/INFORM   01/91 - Pres.

Material Handling Engineering
▲ GO BUSDB: BUSINESS & TRADE JOURNALS   Fixed Span
  Span: 5 yr
▲ GO IQUEST: 1243 (ABI/INFORM) ++   01/92 - Pres.
▲ GO IQUEST: 1615 (TRADE & INDUST. ASAP) ++ 1989 - Pres.
▲ GO KI: BUSI1 (ABI/INFORM)   01/92 - Pres.
▲ GO MRK: ABI/INFORM   01/92 - Pres.

Materials Engineering
▲ GO BUSDB: BUSINESS & TRADE JOURNALS   05/89 - 12/92
  Span: 5 yr
▲ GO IQUEST: 1615 (TRADE & INDUST. ASAP) ++ 1989 - 12/92

Matsushita Weekly (Japan)
GO BUSDB: INDUSTRY NEWSLETTERS   Fixed Span
  Span: 12 mon
GO IQUEST: 2506 (PTS NEWSLETTER DB) +++   10/88 - Pres.

Mature Health
See previous name "AIMplus." See also new name "Solutions for Better Health."
▲ GO HLTDB   10/89 - 04/90
▲ GO IQUEST: 2847 (HLTH PERIODICALS DB) ++ 10/89 - 04/90

▲ - *Selected articles from these periodicals are found online in fulltext. See Section 2 – Focus on Fulltext.*

No Mark - *All articles in these periodicals are found online in fulltext. See Section 2.*

Page 117

Figure 13-1 Use *CompuServe Companion* to find valuable full-text resources on CompuServe

Franklin Partnership through the Ben Franklin Technology Center of Southeastern Pennsylvania. Software may be downloaded at no charge; the use of the service incurs added charges, however.

To use Homework Helper, click on the Connect button and Prodigy will start automatically. Sign on to the system by typing your user name and password. Now, start Homework Helper by clicking on the New Search button.

State your question as a sentence or as keywords. Homework Helper searches for documents that have words and expressions related to your request. To look up an exact phrase or idea, use quotation marks.

Homework Helper returns a list of titles. The title list includes bibliography information (author, title, publisher, and date), the reading grade level (how advanced it is), and a score from 1 to 100 (a high score means the item is a very close match to what you asked for). The titles are ranked, with the closest match at the top of the list. Homework Helper also displays a symbol for each item that tells what type of material it is (book, newspaper, map, and so on).

The title list may be printed. Individual documents can be selected and displayed (downloaded) one at a time, then saved or printed. When Homework Helper shows you an article, it highlights any words in the article that match your request. The closest match is called the "best part" (click on the Best Part button). All close matches in an article are highlighted in yellow on a color monitor.

Homework Helper has additional useful features. Sources (books, newspapers, or magazines) can be selected. Homework Helper automatically checks the spelling of words in the search statement. Advanced Searching permits restricting the search to a particular publication, author, publisher, or time period. The Use Subjects button restricts the search to a particular subject area.

Databases

Prodigy has many databases and menu-driven services that may be useful to the market researcher. Some of these are listed here. Complete listings and descriptions are available in online help files.

- Businessware—software reviews
- Consumer Reports—menu-based access to many areas, including appliances, autos, banking and loans, cameras, computers, foods, home office, product recalls, telephones, and TV/audio/video
- Encyclopedia
- Nexis Advisor
- NYNEX
- Software Guide
- AP Online Business
- Business Headlines
- Business Weekly
- Business/Finance
- Company News
- Company Reports
- D&B Solutions
- Economic Indicators
- Entrepreneur Xchange
- Global View
- Int'l Biz Weekly
- Markets At A Glance
- Price History
- Prodigy For Business
- Quick Business
- U.S. Stocks Update

- World Dollar Update
- World Stocks Update
- World Trade Outlook

America Online

America Online has a very pleasing and easy-to-use graphical interface. However, it is extremely slow. It is very frustrating to wait while the service continually downloads new graphics.

AOL provides many new features and services on a continuous basis. To keep up, I recommend that you go to keywords NEW and WHAT'S HOT frequently to stay current on the latest additions.

AOL's new World Wide Web browser is well integrated with other features. Internet access is not isolated but is available from various subject areas.

Databases

America Online has extensive online resources with graphical content. AOL has many databases grouped in sections and libraries throughout the system. The same databases are frequently available from different subject areas. Some subject areas of interest to the market researcher are listed here.

- Internet Center
- News Search
- Business
- The Newsstand
- Library of Congress
- ASKERIC Online—the ERIC databases

- Barrons' Online
- CNN Newsroom Online
- Compton's Encyclopedia
- C-SPAN Education Services
- NEA Public Forum
- National Public Radio Outreach
- Telecommunications and Networking
- Windows Computing and Software
- The Reference Desk

The Reference Desk is the best area for the business searcher. The best resources from other categories are all available here. The Reference Desk includes the following:

- Internet Gopher and WAIS Databases, including Aeronautics and Astronomy, Agriculture, Anthropology, Arts and Entertainment, Biology, Business and Employment, Census, Chemistry, Computing, Economics and Finance, Education, Engineering, Environment, Geography, Geology and Oceanography, Government and Politics, Library Science, Books and Literature, Networks, and Publishing and Reference.

- Searchable databases, including AOL Directory of Services, Barrons' Booknotes, CNN Newsroom, Computer and Software Companies, Computer Terms Dictionary, C-SPAN, Magazines (such as *Business Week, Compute, Time, Windows, Wired,* and *Worth*), Newsbytes News Network, Newspapers (such as the *Chicago Tribune, Investor's Business Daily,* and *San Jose Mercury News*), News Search, Software File Search, Travel Advisories and Profiles (the U.S. State Department Database), White House Information, Washington Week In Review, and West's Legal Directory—a comprehensive directory of law firms, branch offices, and biographical records of lawyers from the United States and Canada.

The Reference Desk also includes some particularly useful databases for the market researcher. One is Hoover's Business Resources. It consists of the Hoover's Company Profiles database and the Hoover's MasterList. As of March 1995, the Hoover's Company Profiles database includes profiles of approximately 1200 of the largest, most influential, and fastest-growing public and private companies in the world. Profiles include stock information (if a public company), a thumbnail description, key historical events, current officers, address, phone and fax numbers, major products or services, key competitors, and financial data. The Hoover's MasterList database contains information on more than 7800 of the largest and fastest-growing companies in the United States. It complements the Hoover's Company Profiles database by providing more current basic information on each of the profiled companies as well as information on approximately 6500 other major companies not included in the company profile database. Each profile in this database contains the company's name, description, location, phone and fax number, officers' names, sales figures, number of employees, and the company's status (private or public).

> These databases are created and maintained by The Reference Press, Inc., of Austin, Texas (URL: http://www.hoovers.com). Hoover databases are also available on CompuServe and eWorld.

Another particularly useful database is Media Information—especially for tracking the online industry. The Cowles/SIMBA Media Information Network is an online service for the media and information industries. The Cowles/SIMBA Media Information Network is produced by a unit of the Cowles Media Company (a newspaper, magazine, and information services company headquartered in Minneapolis). SIMBA Information, Inc., of Wilton, Connecticut, is responsible for the network. SIMBA is a leading provider of news, analysis, and data on the publishing and media industry. It includes the latest industry news from Cowles/SIMBA Media Daily. Back issues are searchable online. In addition, there are sample issues of SIMBA's newsletters.

Scientific American Online is another very valuable database for the high-technology marketplace. You can search every article published in *Scientific American* since 1948. Access the current issue, search the full text of all back issues through May 1994, or search the annual indexes (abstracts and keywords) for 4,338 feature articles from May 1948 through December 1993. Boolean searches (using AND and OR) are supported for searches by keyword, author name, and date of publication. Back issues and reprints of any article in *Scientific American* are available for a fee.

Summary

In this chapter I have presented descriptions of important (to the researcher) features and databases available on the three major consumer sources—CompuServe, Prodigy, and America Online. Of these features and databases, I believe that Knowledge Index on CompuServe is the most important one. Although it is *for personal use only*, it is the lowest-cost way to learn about searching on professional databases.

All of these services have their own unique features and style; most people use only one as their primary source, because they like the interface or are used to it.

Researchers should be aware that many of the valuable added features on the consumer information services incur a premium, added to the basic monthly fees.

The next chapter gives examples of how to use the consumer services in marketing research.

For Further Reading

1. *CompuServe Companion: Finding Newspapers and Magazines Online* by Glenn S. Orenstein and Ruth M. Orenstein (BiblioData, 1994). As described by the authors, this book is a research aid to find full-text

magazines on CompuServe. Since there are more than 3200 full-text tiles on CompuServe, this represents a large amount of available data to the researcher. Besides locating the sources, the book has useful sections on effective searching, copyright issues, and minimizing cost. If you use CompuServe for research, you should have this book. Contact BiblioData at P.O. Box 61, Needham, MA 02194; 800-247-6553.

2. *The Trail Guide to Prodigy,* by Caroline M. Halliday (Addison-Wesley, 1995). A readable basic guide to using Prodigy. The book covers setting up Prodigy and explores the basics and features. Useful particularly to the beginning user of an online service or as a quick reference to Prodigy features.

3. *The Trail Guide to America Online,* by Jonathan Price (Addison-Wesley, 1995) provides a basic introduction to AOL in an easy-to-read fashion.

4. *Quick Guide to CompuServe,* by Mark K. Billoo (QUE, 1992). A basic, useable introduction to CompuServe.

14

Examples from the Consumer Sources

In this chapter, we assess the effectiveness of the consumer databases for online market research. The test case was run in Prodigy, America Online, and CompuServe.

The Test Case

This is a simple market research request that I will use as an example to demonstrate the marketing research use of online databases. I will follow the basic steps outlined in Chapter 5.

"We're thinking of selling a new product putting Global Positioning System (GPS) receivers in taxis so that taxi companies can track drivers and drivers can find locations. What can you tell me about this?"

The first steps are to define and understand the problem. Now is the time to ask questions to understand what information is really needed. In the real world, this could be a complex problem requiring an industry overview, a detailed listing of potential competitors, and much more. For the example, the information needed is limited to the following:

1. Industry news. What has been written in papers and magazines?

2. A brief company profile of a major GPS manufacturer.

3. A preliminary patent list. Who owns applicable patents?

The next step is to create a list of key words and phrases to use as search terms. As previously shown in Chapter 8, good keywords include: *GPS* or *Global Positioning System; taxis* or *taxicabs; navigate* or *navigation* or *navigating* or *locate* or *location* or *locating;* and *track* or *tracking.* In this example, I specified the name of the manufacturer to profile—Trimble.

Knowledge of sources on the various consumer databases is very important. On the professional databases, there is commonly a method to search many files at once to help determine the proper database. On the consumer sources, searching is generally done one source at a time.

Prodigy

Prodigy has a potentially interesting tool for searching, Homework Helper. Using Homework Helper for this search found no (0) articles for the combinations of *GPS* and *taxi, GPS* and *taxicab,* or *GPS* and *cab.* Searching on *GPS* alone retrieved 150 articles. However, 95 of those articles were not about the Global Positioning System, and 17 were duplicates. The remaining articles were about GPS and could have been read through to see if there was any information on our precise topic—a time-consuming task and not very efficient. On some topics, I would expect Homework Helper to be more helpful than in this case.

Then I used Prodigy to get information about Trimble. For a publicly traded stock like Trimble, excellent and inexpensive results are available. A good recent article (from May 22, 1995) was found about Trimble Navigation, Ltd., and Adobe Systems, Inc., signing a marketing and technology agreement about integrating technologies in a new generation of navigational devices.

Looking in the business report section on Prodigy, I obtained a comprehensive and quite inexpensive Strategic Investor Company Report (from Market Guide, Inc.) on Trimble Navigation, Ltd. This report provides a brief company overview, including name, address, number of employees, and officers' names. We learn that Trimble Navigation, Ltd., designs, manufactures, and markets electronic instruments and systems for determining precise geographic location using the government-funded Global Positioning System.

The report also provided detailed financial information, such as industry rankings, growth rates, revenues, earnings, dividends, price and financial ratios, earnings per share estimates, analyst recommendations, income statements, cash flows, and a balance sheet.

No patent information or patent databases were found.

America Online

AOL provided very little easily accessible information on this topic. A search of fifteen news and magazine databases (one at a time) turned up only a tutorial GPS article from *Scientific American.* No patent information was found.

For Trimble, the previously discussed Hoover's databases provided good basic company information.

If Internet searches are desirable, such as a VERONICA search of Gophers or a WAIS search, they are very easy to accomplish using the friendly AOL interface.

CompuServe

CompuServe has, in IQuest, the most comprehensive access to the professional databases of any of the consumer sources. The search accomplished in the professional databases can be repeated on CompuServe via the gateway. Knowledge Index (GO KI) can also be used to repeat the majority of the search accomplished in the professional databases. (Please observe the personal-use-only limitation on this database.) CompuServe, like AOL, has the Hoover's company databases.

Rather than just repeat the searches accomplished in Chapter 8, I used three of the databases available in CompuServe's Reference Library: Magazine Database Plus, Business Database Plus, and Patent Research Center.

First I looked in Magazine Database Plus. In this database on CompuServe, the search options are

1. Key Words
2. Subject Headings
3. Publication Names
4. Publication Dates
5. Words in Article Text

Selecting option 1, I searched for articles that had the keywords *global positioning system*. I found fifty-five articles with that key phrase (and an additional twenty-three articles with the keyword *GPS*). CompuServe next allows the searcher to

1. Display Article Selection Menu
2. Narrow the Search
3. Undo Last Search Step
4. Start a New Search
5. Display Charge Summary

By selecting choice 2, I can narrow, or focus, the search, using Key Words, Subject Headings, Publication Names, Publication Dates, or Words in Article Text.

I chose Words in Article Text and typed *cab*. The search found one article that matched both search terms above. Now you can display articles, further narrow the search, undo the last step, or start a new search. For the example, I displayed the article, which appears to be potentially useful.

Trucks with brains: the big rigs are rolling better than ever thanks to truckloads of new technology. Popular Mechanics, March 1995 v172 n3, p49(3).

Next I searched in Business Database Plus. Here, you can search business and trade journals for comprehensive, in-depth, company-oriented information or you can search industry newsletters for timely, concise, industry-oriented news and analysis. In Industry Newsletters, I found *GPS Journal* from 1993, but there were no useful articles.

For this example, I searched for the latest news on Trimble in business and trade journals. This database allows searching by Key Words, Subject Headings, Company Names, Publication Names, Publication Dates, or Words in Article Text. I selected Company Names and typed "Trimble." One nice feature of searching in this database is that it now returns a list of names similar to your request, so you may choose the correct company. The result here was the following:

Company Names that contain "Trimble"	*Matches*
1 nelson, Trimble and co.	1
2 pioneer Trimble inc.	1
3 Trimble	1
4 Trimble and associates	1
5 Trimble navigation ltd.	44
6 Trimble west associates	1
7 Trimble western furnishings inc.	1

For Trimble Navigation, the company of interest, forty-four articles were found. Now you can display articles, further narrow the search, undo the last step, or start a new search. I reviewed the articles, finding some particularly applicable to our test search:

1. Cellular fleet tool. Software Industry Report, August 22, 1994

2. Trimble Navigation Ltd. said it would provide PRC Public Sector vehicle tracking and Geographic Information Systems segment of Chicago 911 project. Communications Daily, July 15, 1994

3. Trimble Navigation said it signed contract to be exclusive supplier of mobile satellite data terminals for American

Mobile Satellite Corp. (AMSC) Skycell Fleet Management mobile communications service. Communications Daily, July 8, 1993.

I then used the Patent Research Center to look at GPS patents. The Patent Research Center has US Patents Full Text from 1974, Claims/US Patent Abstracts from 1950, Derwent World Patents Index from 1960, and JAPIO (Japanese patents) from 1976. This area also has a useful tool that allows you to look at all four individual databases simultaneously and inexpensively: Scan all the above databases. For this example, I used Scan and this search statement (for this system, "/" is the truncation operator):

(GPS OR GLOBAL POSITION/ SYSTEM/) AND (TAXI/ OR TAXICAB/ OR CAB/)

The results are listed next. For additional charges, each of the individual databases may be searched to obtain the desired patents. (The same patent probably appears in several databases.) Because of the large number of hits, the search should also be narrowed by adding additional terms such as *navigate* or *navigation* or *navigating* or *locate* or *location* or *locating;* and *track* or *tracking.*

	Results	Format
Claims/US Pat Abs (1950–1970)	0	abstract
Claims/US Pat Abs (1971–1981)	0	abstract
Claims/US Pat Abs (1982–date)	14	abstract
Claims/US Pat Abs Weekly	1	abstract
Derwent Wld Pat Idx (1963–80)	212	abstract
Derwent Wld Pat Idx (1981–)	830	abstract
JAPIO	19	abstract
U.S. Patents Fulltext (1971–79)	2	full text
U.S. Patents Fulltext (1980–89)	30	full text
U.S. Patents Fulltext (90–date)	165	full text

Summary

Limited secondary marketing research can be performed using the consumer databases. CompuServe has the best selection of databases for the researcher. AOL is not very useful but has very easy-to-use access to searching the Internet. Prodigy has excellent public company reports at a low price. CompuServe offers gateway access to many professional databases, for more comprehensive searching.

I still strongly recommend that anyone who must obtain high-quality data in a limited time get full access to one or more professional databases. However, for the occasional searcher or for the once-in-a-while market research task, I would recommend CompuServe, because it provides useful access to a very broad range of data.

15 | *How to Keep Up*

A major problem for market researchers and information professionals is keeping up with the location, cost, and accessibility of all the available information. Staying current is necessary in order to provide the best, most timely, and most cost-effective marketing research.

In this chapter I discuss some of the methods and tools I use to attempt to stay abreast of the information environment. I use alert services (current awareness or SDI) and information management software. And I read—a lot!

The Problem: An Information Explosion

I was recently asked about "The Information Explosion." As I tried to define the problem, I found that

- There are 500,000 usable words in English now, versus 125,000 words in Shakespeare's time.
- The number of books available in top libraries has doubled in fourteen years.
- 9600 periodicals are released each day in the United States.
- 1000 books are released each day worldwide.
- More information has been created in the last thirty years than in the previous 5000 years.
- Available information doubles every five years (and the rate is increasing).

- From 1975 through 1994, the number of online databases increased from 301 to 8776, and the number of records increased from 52 million to 6.3 billion.
- Pick any figure you want for the number of Internet users—but we all agree that growth is phenomenal.

Without some sort of disciplined approach, keeping up is impossible. In fact, a major problem in writing this book was keeping up with changes during the writing process.

Thinking about Solutions

There is no magic solution—I have not found any methods that do not require time and effort. However, I do follow a disciplined process that allows me to keep up with the majority of the changes, including

- Using inexpensive alert services to highlight important information. These provide automatic information selection and downloading. They are available on the Internet and from both consumer and professional databases.
- Using information management software. I use both specialized tools and one of the many commercially available database programs. I create and maintain a searchable file of information sources.
- Reading selected magazines, newspapers, and newsletters. I also attend conferences, seminars, courses, and meetings.

Although using my exact methods is not necessary, I believe (and strongly recommend) that using each of the three elements I use will allow anyone to keep up, with a minimum of time and effort.

Alert Services

Many commercial and professional companies offer alert services. All of the major professional database services allow you to set up an automated program that will repeat a search in specified databases at specified intervals and list new information. Companies such as Individual, Inc., provide services that deliver headlines on specified topics by fax every day. The *Wall Street Journal* offers a customized online version of its paper to allow easy access to just the information you want.

I have found that the best deal for me in this area is to use two services found on CompuServe: the Executive News Service (GO ENS) and PC Magazine Newswatch (GO ZNT:EDITOR).

I use the Executive News Service (ENS) to monitor stories from the Associated Press newswires, Dow Jones, PR NewsWire, the *Washington Post*, United Press International, and Reuters newswires for stories containing information about online or about the Internet. The stories are clipped as they come across the wires and held in an electronic folder for me to review at my convenience (about every other day).

ENS allows fairly complicated search statements and multiple folders, so you may set up the system in many different ways. Type up to seven separate search terms or search term combinations and ENS will look for this information in each story released on the news sources you have marked. You can include a plus sign (+) to represent AND, a minus sign (–) to represent NOT, and a vertical bar symbol (|) to represent OR. Use parentheses ( ) to determine the order of processing. An asterisk (*) can be used to signify a wild card at the beginning or end of a search term. For example, "COMPUT*" will find stories with the word *compute, computer, computers, computation,* and so forth.

ENS is a very powerful and relatively inexpensive tool. Recent articles appearing in my folder have included the following:

- ORLANDO, Fla., April 30 /PRNewswire/—The Orlando Sentinel Online has become a reality, bringing Central Florida news and information as close as a computer to more than two million America Online subscribers.
- SEATTLE, April 30 (Reuter)—Starwave Corp., one of Microsoft Corp <MSFT.O> cofounder Paul Allen's multimedia companies, expands its presence on the Internet Monday with the launch of Mr. Showbiz, an online entertainment magazine.
- AUCKLAND, May 1 (Reuter)—The Asian Development Bank (ADB) marked its annual general meeting by going live on the Internet on Monday.
- TOKYO—Japan's Internet population is still small—at least for now. About 72,400 host computers have connected to the global computer network, placing the country 40th in the rankings for Internet penetration, when measured in correlation with GNP.
- NEW YORK, May 1 /PRNewswire/—Profound, Inc. today announced immediate availability of its new Windows(R)-based online business intelligence service, Profound(TM), which provides access to the most comprehensive business database ever developed, with global market and industry news, research, company and broker information, and up-to-the-minute news.
- SANTA CRUZ, Calif., May 1 /PRNewswire/—THE NET-CENTER, The Center of the Internet, today announced it has been chosen as a distributor of the new Spry "Air Mosaic" and Internet-On-A-Disk.
- DAYTON, Ohio, May 1 (Reuter)—Online service provider Lexis-Nexis and the New York Times Co's information services unit said Lexis-Nexis will offer the current day's news from the Times newspaper in addition to its archive service.

The other very useful tool I use on CompuServe is PC Magazine Newswatch (GO ZNT:EDITOR). PC Magazine Newswatch provides computer industry news as reported in the mainstream press, compiled by Tom Giebel, technical associate at *PC Magazine.* It can be read online or downloaded and used with any word processor. A few typical results from April 26, 1995, are shown here:

- Computer industry continues to show robust growth even as the rest of the economy appears to slow. The networking boom and the availability of cheap and powerful multimedia systems are pumping up company earnings. [WSJ 4/19 p.B4]

- Microsoft acquisition of Intuit should be approved or denied by the Justice Dept. around May 1, now that the two companies have fulfilled all the Dept's requests for information. Antitrust experts say it is likely the acquisition will be challenged. [WSJ 4/21 p.B4]

- Microsoft antitrust case: a panel of federal appeals court judges said that Judge Sporkin may have overstepped his authority in rejecting the Justice Dept. settlement. Comments indicate the panel may not completely reject or uphold Sporkin's decision, but give the case back to Sporkin with specific more direction on how to handle it. [WSJ 4/25 p.B7] [NYT 4/24 p.D1] Microsoft and Justice defend settlement. [NYT 4/25 p.D5]

- Kevin Mitnick should have computer fraud charges against him dropped, says his lawyer, because of an illegal search warrant. [NYT 4/21 p.D8]

- Computer nerds are basking in newfound admiration as society embraces technology. Today's nerds aren't just creating new technology for kicks: they also want to make lots of money. [USA 4/20 p.1b]

- Passwords proliferate life in the digital age, and people are being forced to remember scores of secret codes for everything from on-line services to burglar alarms. Security experts offer password management tips. [WSJ 4/19 p.A1]

America Online provides access to products and news from the Cowles/SIMBA Media Information Network—an online service for the media and information industries. It includes the latest industry news, as reported in the Cowles/SIMBA Media Daily, the news areas of Inside Media Online, and Direct NewsLine. In addition, there are sample issues of SIMBA's newsletters, an area for user contributions, and a message board that covers virtually every facet of media and information. This area is worth visiting on a regular basis.

An alert service provides a great deal of help in keeping up. I expect various of these services will continue to proliferate. An information specialist or market researcher will find that one or more of these alert services are important aids in keeping up.

Monitoring the Internet

Keeping up with the rapidly expanding Internet can be a full-time job. Luckily there are also valuable tools on the Internet to help. First, I use the alert services just described to monitor Internet news. Then there are resources on the Internet I regularly access.

The Ziff-Davis Publishing Company home page, http://www. ziff.com, provides access to all of the Ziff-Davis magazines, such as *PC Magazine* and *Interactive Week*, plus news stories about computers and the Internet. I visit here frequently to review the new information, much of which is searchable and downloadable.

The Whole Internet Catalog, http://nearnet.gnn.com/gnn/ wic/index.html, is another outstanding site I regularly visit. The Whole Internet Catalog offers choices such as What's New and the Top 25. It also allows searching: All Subjects and All Catalog Entries—including E-Zines, Newspapers, Internet Commerce, Small Business, Libraries, Indexes to U.S. Government Resources, Sites of the Day, and What's New Pages.

Several mailing lists provide valuable and up-to-date information about the Internet. One I like very much is Tech-Link, a free E-mail newsletter about CMP's TechWeb. TechWeb is located at http://techweb.cmp.com/techweb and is updated every day. On the site you will find current issues of sixteen CMP publications (including *Interactive Age, Net-Guide, Information Week*, and *Windows* magazine)—as well as the ability to search more than a year of back issues free. New content includes daily news updates, contests, and other special editorial features.

Another good source is the Internet Marketing discussion mailing list. This list has ongoing discussions about marketing on the Internet, which offer a continuous update on new issues. For information about the list, send E-mail with the words INFO INTERNET-MARKETING to LISTPROC@POPCO.COM or look on the World Wide Web at http://www.popco.com/.

In an example of the changing Internet environment, the list moderator for Internet Marketing has asked for a voluntary subscription fee. Running such a list requires both time and money. If people are to continue performing moderator (or other) tasks, I expect this to be a necessary trend.

There is simply no complete guide to new resources. Two good resources, however, are the Netlink server and the Net-Happenings list.

1. Access To New Net Resource Sites—
   gopher:// liberty.uc. wlu.edu/—then select Netlink Server and Recent Additions.

2. Net-Happenings—A keyword index and a WAIS full-text index are available at http://www-iub.indiana.edu/cgi-bin/nethaps/.

Reading

Selecting and reading a few magazines or newsletters is an important part of keeping up. Valuable sources include computer magazines, business magazines, local papers, the *New York Times*, and the *Wall Street Journal*. In addition, specialized magazines and newsletters such as the ones listed here provide timely and accessible information.

- *Searcher*, published ten times a year by Learned Information, Inc. (609-654-6266).

- *Database* and *Online*, each published six times a year by Online, Inc. (203-761-1466).

- *Information Broker*, published six times a year by Burwell Enterprises, Inc. (713-537-9051)

- *The Information Advisor*, published monthly by FIND/SVP (212-645-4500). The January 1995 issue was a special edition entitled *Tackling Information Overload.*

- *CD ROM Professional*, published by Pemberton Press (800-222-3766, ext. 517. In Connecticut, call 203-761-1466, ext. 517). It provides CD-ROM information for the professional user.

- *American Demographics* (800-365-0688). Published monthly by American Demographics, Inc.

- *Internet Business Advantage*, a monthly newsletter published by The Cobb Group Media, Inc. (800-223-8720).

- *Internet World*, a magazine published by Meckler Corporation (E-mail: meckler@jvnc.net; phone: 800-MECKLER).

- *Online Access* (E-mail: 70324.343@compuserve.com).

Although not strictly reading, another valuable method for keeping up is going to conferences (such as National Online and Online), courses, and seminars. Professional societies such as the American Marketing Association, Association of Independent Information Professionals, and the Special Libraries Association all sponsor valuable meetings, seminars, and courses.

Information Managers and Databases

One major concern is keeping track of all this information input once it's been obtained. Information can be gathered in a variety of forms: paper, electronic documents, E-mail messages, files from online services, faxed documents, or newspaper and magazine articles. A reliable system of organization and maintenance is necessary. Commercial databases and information management software can help.

"Document image managers" is one among a category of programs that are very useful. These programs provide scanning, optical character recognition (OCR), indexing, searching, retrieving, and printing of documents. Such software is in its infancy and is still improving—it is slow and, in my experience, causes random system crashes. Some of the programs in this category are Watermark, FileMagic Plus, PageKeeper, ImageFast, Fileflo, Recollect, Equip+, Concordance, and PaperClip.

> A good reference on these programs is "Document Image Managers" by David Seachrist, in the May 1995 issue of *BYTE* magazine.

The information management program I currently use is called PageKeeper, from Caere. PageKeeper can

- Scan and perform OCR on paper.
- Read electronic information.
- Index information stored in a PageKeeper database and other computer files.
- Retrieve relevant information with a built-in search engine. PageKeeper uses its indexes to find information—and rank it in order of relevance. Three different search methods are available: Word Search, Boolean Search, and Similar Document Search.

One problem with searches on PageKeeper: only the document is identified in a search. If you store and index long documents, it may be difficult to find the location of search terms within a document. The solution is to break long documents into sections (chapters, topics, and so on) and store them that way.

As any of us tracks information resources, we end up with long lists or bulging files showing the locations of great information resources. Then we (at least I) cannot find them easily. The solution—using any database program you are comfortable with—is to create a sortable list on your own computer. The newest versions of databases are powerful, yet still simple and easy to use.

For example, I review and collect many Uniform Resource Locators (URLs) for valuable Internet sites. I have created a database using two fields—URL and Description—for that information. I then use the sort function to alphabetize the listing and remove duplicates. (Other fields could be added to categorize or comment on the sites.) I then save the file as a comma-separated file. Using my HTML authoring software (HTML Assistant Pro), I next automatically convert that list to HTML—it's now ready to run from my home page. I then use my home page as my Internet search tool. Another useful trick for remembering web sites is to print a copy of the first page of each site and keep it in a three-ring binder.

Specialized databases are also becoming available for searching and maintaining Internet information resources. Ecco Software offers a program called the ECCO Internet Address Book. Contact Ecco at 206-885-4272, ext. 29, for more information. Another similar useful example is VIZION from SIRSI (E-mail vizinfo@sirsi.com for more information). It is a search tool, an organizer, a contact manager with speed-dial connections to the Internet, and a customizable database of online information sources.

VIZION lets you conduct a search offline to find information on World Wide Web home pages, modem-accessed bulletin boards, FTP sites, Gopher servers, Telnet hosts, and Z39.50 libraries. VIZION currently operates under Microsoft Windows; versions for Apple Macintosh and UNIX X Windows will be available.

The powerful search tools included in VIZION allow searching by title, description, abstract, and keywords. You can also sort and filter destinations for attributes such as location (state or country), institution type (government, university, store, and so on), service that supplies the destination (bulletin board, Internet provider, magazine, and others) and the main subject.

You can manage and customize VIZION's database to create your own "contact manager" for online information sources. Add new destinations to the database by typing or copying the information from the sources as you find them.

Summary

There is no magic—effort is required to stay up-to-date. The first step in keeping up with information important to your business is to allocate time, at least once a week, preferably more often. Second, select the tools to help you. As I discussed in this chapter, I use custom databases and online alert services, and I read a lot. The process includes

- Using inexpensive alert services to highlight important information. These provide automatic information selection and downloading. They are available on the Internet and from both consumer and professional databases.
- Using information management software. I use both specialized tools and one of the many commercially available database programs. I create and maintain a searchable file of information sources.

- Reading selected magazines, newspapers, and newsletters and attending conferences, seminars, courses, and meetings.

Using each of these three elements will allow anyone to keep up with a minimum of time and effort.

The tools, techniques, and discipline used to monitor the information explosion are also valuable when you are performing ongoing market research—tracking customers, competitors, and the overall marketplace.

Finally, to keep up with my opinions about valuable Internet resources, visit my home page at http://www.vivamus.com.

Another reference on this topic is the January 1995 issue of *The Information Advisor*, entitled "Tackling Information Overload." Contact Find/SVP at 212-645-4500 for more information about this useful newsletter.

16 | *Data Quality—The Researcher's Responsibilities*

Never Bet Your House on a Single Information Source

In this chapter I will discuss an important responsibility of the information professional or market researcher: dealing with data errors. All data you obtain may have errors, such as these:

- The original data may be wrong.
- The data may have been entered into the database incorrectly.
- Data may be indexed or stored incorrectly.
- Data may be missing.

I will explore issues affecting the accuracy or quality of data, the effects of misspellings, data collection and verification, the importance of original sources, timeliness, and completeness.

Assessing the quality of data from the Internet and from newsgroups, forums, or other online discussion groups is particularly difficult.

Spelling and Other Errors

Misspelling happens—spelling errors probably most frequently result from the manual input of material into databases. (This is frequently done overseas with non-English-speaking workers.) As more and more documents are produced electronically, this problem may subside. However, even with spell-checking software, spelling errors will exist in the original documents. For an example of a typical spelling error, look at reference 16 in "For Further Reading"—there is a misspelling in the title of an article about database quality.

Another major error associated with misspelling or keyboarding is inconsistency. One common example of this sort is found when attempting to obtain all the articles associated with a particular company. DIALOG has a very useful file that allows you to look up companies in all the files. The Company Name Finder file finds all the different spellings of a company name used in all the different databases. I looked up John Deere: some of the variations are shown in Table 16-1. To obtain all the information available on John Deere, you must look at all these different spellings.

A third issue is consistency in indexing. Documents are indexed and assigned keywords (called *descriptors* on DIALOG) that aid the searcher in finding documents about specific topics. If different documents are indexed by different people at different times (over a period of many years, in some databases), differences do occur. The professional researcher must be aware of such a problem and expand the search by using variations on terms.

Consistency problems can also be caused by changes in names of publications. For a complete search, more than one journal name may be required.

For example, to obtain a bibliography of database quality issues, I used several descriptor terms to describe the industry of interest—*information* and *database*—retrieving all phrases that had the word *information* or *database*. Documents were retrieved indexed by information industry, information services, government information, and so on.

Table 16-1
Inconsistencies in a
Company's Name

Number of Records	Spelling
36	John Deere
15	Deere
8	John Deere Co
5	Deere (John)
4	John Deere & Co
4	John Deere Company
2	John Deere Company Division
2	John Deere Tractors
2	John Deer Co
2	Deere (US)
1	John Deer Tractor Co
1	John Deere & Company
1	John Deere Company // Deere & Company
1	John Deere Inc
1	John Deere Incorporated
1	John Deere Tractor Company
1	John Deere Tractor Works
1	John Deere Tractor Works // Deere And Co
1	John Deere Tractors & Equipment
1	Deere &
1	Deere & C

Although there was significant overlap in the terms, this method reduced errors due to inconsistent indexing. The penalty is the generation of undesired results (called false hits). Out of 140 titles, 20 good references were found.

Translations and foreign terms (such as British words: *centre* versus *center*) can create additional problems. If translated databases (such as JAPIO for Japanese patents) are important to the research project, the professional researcher must become familiar with language idiosyncrasies.

When you are using nonprofessional sources such as the Internet, some of these problems are not very important yet: Internet search tools are too immature. As search tools improve, these issues, particularly spelling and consistency, will become increasingly important. For example, after carefully submitting my World Wide Web home page to an Internet index, I could not find it using that index: I had misspelled my own company name in the submittal.

Consistency also becomes very important when you are using multiple search tools to obtain maximum information. The same search using different tools may obtain very different results. Relevance ranking tools such as LEXIS-NEXIS FREESTYLE provide a different result than a Boolean search on the same database.

Collection and Verification Methods

Database producers obtain information in many ways. Some databases are the result of copying magnetic computer tape provided by the data source. Many patent databases are of this type. Standard computer verification methods are used to ensure data validity.

Hard-copy information (such as documents and magazines) are inputted by keyboarding or by scanning and using OCR. Quality verification methods include hand comparison of selected samples, spell-checking, and indexing documents twice and combining the results.

Some database producers use interviews and phone calls to obtain data (particularly for hard-to-find information like private company financial information). Verification is very difficult in these cases because the interview subject may lie. Database producers attempt to obtain information from multiple sources and review the results for consistency—but these databases have the potential for the highest error rate.

Internet data sources can be a particular problem. Data may be placed on the Internet by anyone, and the data could have errors that were not found since no quality control exists—

or, even worse, the data could be deliberately false. Special care must be taken with data obtained from the Internet.

Market researchers and information professionals must be aware of the way data is collected and verified on the sources they use. Ask your vendors questions!

Original Sources—Identification and Access

The more important the data is to a decision, the more important it is to validate and verify that data. One way is to obtain the data from multiple sources. However, this will not help when the original data is wrong.

Though it is not often necessary to find and access the original source material, the best databases make that process easy by providing complete and correct bibliographic information for all source material. If your key piece of information comes from a single source, it may be necessary to verify the information. As previously discussed, for one client, I contacted the author of an important article and obtained information that significantly changed the results.

When using data from the Internet or various discussion groups, find out the source of the information. Determine for yourself the source validity—verify the credentials and biases of the persons providing the information. Since much information in these sources comes second- and thirdhand, significant effort can be required to validate information. In one case, I sent twenty-two E-mail messages over a week's time to get an answer—so much for instant information access.

Timeliness

Another important attribute of high-quality data is timeliness. For market research, the most up-to-date data is required. Though many databases are updated regularly (daily or weekly), there is always some lag in obtaining information. You must be aware of the timeliness of data provided and know where to obtain the most timely information. Online information access is becoming more timely as more newspapers and magazines are published using computer technology: some sources are available online before they reach the newsstand.

Even when information is provided rapidly, there are still significant lags—the story in this week's magazine may have been written several weeks earlier. Remember: the most up-to-date information is still in someone's head!

Database producers do not always update or deliver information as often as they claim. I have selected a few examples of this problem, as shown in Table 16-2. There may be good reasons for delays, but the searcher must be aware of the database's timeliness. Most professional information services provide information on the latest update of each database.

Table 16-2
Not All Databases Meet Their Update Schedules*

Database	Scheduled Update Frequency	Actual Update Status on May 30, 1995	Overdue
D&B—Dun's International Market Identifiers	Quarterly	1994/Q4	2 quarters
D&B—Dun's Market Identifiers	Monthly	January 1995	4 months
Books In Print	Monthly	December 1994	5 months
UPI News	Daily	May 23, 1994	372 days
Buyer's Guide to Micro Software	Monthly	September 1993	20 months
Drug Information—Full	Quarterly	May 1994	4 quarters
Unlisted Drugs	Monthly	December 1993	17 months
Standards and Specifications	Monthly	June 1993	23 months

*Databases are from DIALOG Information Services

Another timeliness issue of concern is the existence of closed databases. These databases may still have valuable data, but they are not being updated. For example, on DIALOG, the Bible, an encyclopedia, a quotations database, and Nuclear Science Abstracts are closed databases. The searcher must know which databases are closed.

Again, since update schedules and update times are not always available when you are searching nonprofessional databases, special care must be taken.

Completeness

Data completeness is also important. Not all vendors provide exactly the same data. Not all articles are covered from each journal, and not the same ranges of dates are covered. For example, a marketing newsletter, *Marketing Research Review*, is provided in complete full text in the PTS Newsletter database and is partially covered (selected articles) in PROMT. The starting date of coverage varies from October 1985 on NewsNet to October 1991 on DIALOG to December 1991 on Dow Jones.

Do not expect data completeness from the nonprofessional sources or for very old data. Some data is just not available online and must be obtained from libraries.

Security and Rumors

An important issue with respect to data found on the Internet is deliberately false information or rumors, which propagate easily throughout the Internet.

Anyone may post data on the Internet, and the source of data is not always clearly identified. Another potential problem is that data might be changed. Not all data on the Internet is secure against modification by malicious or mischievous people.

I have not encountered a specific example of these problems yet, but the potential obviously exists. I again strongly recommend that all data found be checked for validity. This is particularly true for information found on the Internet.

Summary

In this chapter I discussed issues affecting the accuracy and quality of data. Quality assessment of data from the Internet and data from newsgroups, forums, or other online discussion groups was shown to be particularly difficult. Data errors discussed included the following:

- Errors in the original information source
- Data-entry errors
- Incorrect data indexing or storage
- Missing data

The research professional must be aware of all possible problems with any research results and take appropriate steps to minimize any impact. The professional should know the following information for the databases used:

- Periods covered—number of records by year
- Time since last update
- Source coverage—names and indexing of journals
- Content by record type—full text, bibliographic, citation, abstract, and so on

Multiple sources should be utilized where appropriate. Original sources or authors should be contacted for critical information. Reports should include statements warning the end user of any potential issues and an assessment of data quality.

For Further Reading

I have listed here a new book on this topic (reference 2) and the sources I read in preparing to write this chapter. Many of these references are very well written and will be of significant value to someone interested in learning more.

1. "Beyond Information Quality: Fitness for Purpose and Electronic Information Resource Use," by Jane E. Klobas, *Journal of Information Science* 21, no. 2 (March–April): p. 995.

2. *Electronic Information Delivery: Ensuring Quality and Value,* edited by Reva Basch (Gower, 1995). ISBN 0-566-07567-9.

3. "CIQM's Second Report—The Centre for Information Quality Management's Report on Project to Ensure Database Quality for UK Libraries," *Searcher* 3, no. 4 (April 1995): p. 22.

4. "Quality of Information—Part II," by Tom Valovic, *Telecommunications* 29, no. 2 (February 1995): p. 8.

5. "CIQM: Report on Database Quality," by Chris Armstrong, *Database* 17, no. 6 (December 1994): p. 45.

6. "Towards A New Metric: 'Quality of Information,'" by Tom Valovic, *Telecommunications* 28, no. 7 (July 1994): p. 8.

7. "Testing Database Quality," by Pamela Cahn, *Database* 17, no. 1 (February 1994): p. 23.

8. "Searching for Skeletons in the Database Cupboard, Part II: Errors of Commission," by Peter Jacso, *Database* 16, no. 2 (April 1993): pp. 30–36.

9. "Frequency and Impact of Spelling Errors in Bibliographic Data Bases," by Charles P. Bourne, *Information Processing and Management* 13, no. 1 (1977): pp. 1–12.

10. "AL Aside—Ideas: The Dirty Database Test," *American Libraries* 22, no. 3 (March 1991): p. 197.

11. "Caveat Searcher: Spelling Bees Abuzzing," *Database Searcher* 7, no. 5 (June 1991): p. 38.

12. "The Catalogers' 'Invisible College' at Work: The Case of the Dirty Database Test," by Jim Dwyer, *Cataloging and Classification Quarterly* 14, no. 1 (1991): pp. 75–82.

13. "The Most Popular Databases," by Carol Tenopir, *Library Journal* 116 (April 1, 1991): pp. 96–98.

14. "Measuring the Quality of the Data: Report on the Fourth Annual SCOUG Retreat," by Reva Basch, *Database Searcher* 6, no. 8 (October 1990): pp. 18–24.

15. "Quality Requirements for Databases—Project for Evaluating Finnish Databases," by R. Juntunen et al., pp. 351–359 in *Online Information 91: Proceedings of the 15th International Online Information Meeting,* London, 10–12 December (Oxford: Learned Information, 1991).

16. "Searching for Skeletons in the Database Cupboard, Part I: Errors of Omission," by Peter Jacso, *Database* 16, no. 1 (February 1993): pp. 38–49.

17. "The Linear File: A Proposal for Database 'Nutrition and Ingredient' Labeling," by Peter Jacso, *Database* 16, no. 1 (February 1993): pp. 7–9.

18. "The Essence of Quality for Information Companies," by Marydee Ojala, *Information World Review* 82 (June 1993): pp. 18–19.

17 | *Document Delivery: Now and the Future*

An important part of online marketing research is obtaining the information once it has been found. Documents are available from document-delivery services, as full text online, by facsimile, or by E-mail. Online services are advancing document delivery capabilities: the new Profound service provides full-color output from some sources using Acrobat Reader from Adobe Systems.

This is an evolving and improving area. Technological advances will lead to quick delivery of full images over the Internet.

This chapter briefly discusses the various document-delivery methods and comments on future trends.

Copyright issues are discussed in Chapter 18.

etting the Documents

Document-delivery firms are one source for documents. These firms have rapid access to original source documents via their own holdings or by close working relationships with major libraries. One such firm is Information Express (3250 Ash Street, Palo Alto, CA 94306; 415-494-8787, fax: 415-494-6541; service@express.com or http://www.express. com).

Founded in 1985, Information Express specializes in fast, competitively priced delivery of technical articles for all industries. Information Express is also the document supplier for the IAC and Predicasts databases. Information Express provides full-service document delivery through the use of four types of sources:

- **Holdings List.** Includes core journals covering pharmaceutical, engineering, computer science, and business industries. Articles from the internal holdings list are sent out in one day.

- **California Sources.** The Stanford University and the University of California library systems. Up to 75 percent of articles from these sources are filled in one day, and 90 percent are filled in forty-eight hours.

- **Special Sources.** Linda Hall, National Library of Medicine, Canada Institute for Scientific and Technical Information, special conference proceedings collection.

- **Outside Sources.** Publishers, authors, associations, and other vendors.

Information Express provides a searchable Journal Index and a Table of Contents Alert service on its Web page.

A few of the many other document-delivery firms include Associated Information Consultants, University Microfilms International (UMI) Article Clearing House, Engineering Societies Library, Information On Demand, Infocus Research Services, Information Store, and Dynamic Information.

Full-Text Databases

The quickest way to obtain information online is by using full-text sources. More than 5000 journals, newspapers, newsletters, newswires, and radio/TV transcripts are available online in full text. Text is available, but photographs, illustrations, graphs, and many tables are not included.

The best way to locate full-text sources online is to use Bib-lioData's *Fulltext Sources Online*—available in print and online (BiblioData, P.O. Box 61, Needham Heights, MA 02194; 617-444-1154, fax: 617-449-4584). Use it as your first step in any full-text online search to pinpoint which databases have a specific journal, newspaper, newsletter, or newswire in full text.

Fulltext Sources Online covers all topics, including science, technology, medicine, law, finance, business, industry, and newspapers. Online hosts included are DataStar, BRS, DIALOG, DataTimes, Dow Jones, Genios, Europeene des Donnees, FT Profile, Infomat, Info Globe, NEXIS, LEXIS, NewsNet, QL, Reuter Textline, STN, Vu/Text, and Westlaw.

Image Databases

Local image databases, either on tape or on CD-ROM, provide very prompt document delivery. Many firms and libraries have this service available. It is likely that most databases in the future will have image storage and retrieval.

Electronic Delivery

Electronic delivery of documents is becoming available from multiple sources. UMI (800-521-0600, ext. 2786) provides fax and Internet delivery of documents.

Knight-Ridder Information (DIALOG and DataStar) has been delivering patents (U.S. and European) and ABI/Inform articles by fax since 1994. KR is now introducing extended document delivery service options, including many more sources (more than 500,000 journal titles, 3 million books, 4 million reports, 300,000 conference proceedings, and 500,000 theses).

Orders can be placed by telephone, fax, E-mail, or online. Delivery is available by mail, express, courier, or fax. Image delivery will be available through the Internet.

UnCover (discussed in Chapter 11) is accessible at http://www.carl.org/uncover/unchome.html. UnCover offers the opportunity to order fax copies of articles from the database. To order an article from the UnCover database, perform a search to locate the article you want and mark the article. Once you have marked all of the articles you wish to order, order the articles by following the on-screen directions. Articles will be delivered directly to your fax machine as fast as twenty-four hours. Costs for delivery (including copyright fees) are displayed on-screen and can be paid with a credit card or a deposit account.

Summary

Document delivery is one of the last steps in fulfilling a research task—the delivery of the research results and the report. Documents are currently delivered via full-text databases or through a document-delivery service. Documents arrive online, by fax, or by mail.

Two major trends are visible in the document-delivery process. First, document-delivery firms are combining into relatively few large firms. Major professional services such as DIALOG are investing heavily in document delivery. At the end of the shakeout, a few very large full-service document-delivery firms will dominate.

The other major trend is image delivery online. New software such as Adobe Acrobat (available now on Profound), Xpressnet, and Ariel provide full image transmission over the Internet or other online channels. In the near future, I expect online image delivery to be the most common delivery method.

18 | *Legal, Ethical, and Intellectual Property*

This chapter discusses the controversial issues of copyright online, electronic distribution rights of authors, export laws, and the Internet. It also reviews other legal and ethical issues associated with the online services.

The Copyright Laws

Copyright is an important issue for the future of online information. The professional services have well-established copyright procedures in place. In general, the consumer databases also have established procedures for protecting intellectual property.

The Internet is the site of the largest battles. On one side are the authors and artists who rightly believe that they should be compensated for their efforts. At the other extreme are the "information has a right to be free" true believers. Solutions for intellectual property protection must be achieved to ensure the maximum availability of information.

The best source for basic copyright law information is your local library. Copyright information is also easily obtainable from the U.S. Copyright Office (Library of Congress, Washington, DC 20559-6000). You can telephone the Copyright Office (from 8:30 A.M. to 5:00 P.M., Eastern time, Monday through Friday) at 202-707-3000 to speak to a copyright information specialist and order documentation. A brief overview of copyright law is provided at the end of this chapter.

Pamela Samuelson, a professor of law at the University of Pittsburgh, has provided a great deal of information about intellectual property issues in her paper "Legally Speaking: The NII Intellectual Property Report" published in the December 1994 issue of *Communications of the ACM*. In this report she reviews and strongly disagrees with recommendations made in the *NII Intellectual Property Report*.

We all agree that authors and publishers of creative works need reasonable assurance that their intellectual property rights will be respected. Digital network environments (like the Internet) are a particular problem because of the ease of making multiple copies and distributing them.

However, Samuelson feels that the government's suggestions in the report are excessive and unnecessary. These suggestions include

- Making digital transmission of a copy of a copyrighted work a copyright infringement
- Abolishing a purchaser's right now granted under the "first sale" rule for works distributed by digital transmission. (This rule allows a person to read a book and then give it to a friend.)

Paying Copyright Fees

Charges for viewing and downloading documents on the professional and consumer services include the payment of copyright. When documents are obtained from a document-delivery firm, copyright fees are charged. In general, a document may be delivered and an archival copy may be kept. Any additional copies must have copyright fees paid.

The researcher should note that most information online is copyrighted—marking is not required since March 1, 1987. Government information is not copyrighted (but a specific collection or format of that data may be). Treat all information as if it were copyrighted.

Primary issues that exist in these cases are dealing with multiple copies (for a meeting, for example) and dealing with copies made available by electronic distribution (on an internal network, for example). There are many solutions.

Knight-Ridder DIALOG has a system called Electronic Redistribution and Archiving (ERA). While searching on DIALOG, you can order additional copies, purchase the right to make additional paper or electronic copies on your own, or purchase the right to electronically store (archive) information from participating DIALOG databases in your company's in-house system.

The DIALOG ERA service also provides an option to report additional copies or archival rights after your initial request. This "after-the-fact" feature allows you to pay copyright fees for records you have copied or archived anytime after the original output arrives.

Redistribution pricing is very simple. Take the standard DIALOG price of the format designated and multiply it by a pricing multiplier that is determined by the number of "copies" requested. The ARCHIVE option has a different multiplier table because it is based on the number of employees in your organization who will have access to the archived data.

Another important organization for dealing with copyright fees is the Copyright Clearance Center (CCC, 222 Rosewood Drive, Danvers, MA 01923; 508-750-8400, fax: 508-750-4744). CCC provides a full portfolio of copyright licensing services to organizations. CCC is a not-for-profit corporation formed at the suggestion of Congress to facilitate copyright compliance. The services provided are the following:

- The Annual Authorizations Service (AAS) provides the option of paying a single annual fee to corporations. By paying an annual fee, licensees eliminate the burdens of seeking individual permissions from publishers as well as tracking, reporting, and paying fees for individual copying acts.

- Another service is the Academic Permissions Service (APS). When making academic course packs and classroom handouts, educators can use the APS as a centralized system for managing permissions and royalties.

- The Transactional Reporting Service (TRS) provides users with immediate authorization to make photocopies from more than 1.7 million publications from more than 9000 publishers worldwide. TRS customers do not have to make individual fee payments to publishers, but instead deal with CCC.

CCC, through bilateral agreements with its foreign counterparts, also provides licensed access to the world's published works.

The Electronic Copyright

A continuing controversy about information placed on online sources is the compensation of authors for electronic distribution for their work. Currently many authors feel that they have not authorized electronic (online) distribution and they are not being compensated. Various lawsuits against magazines, database vendors, and online services are in progress. According to a press release dated May 18, 1995, an author's registry organization (with nearly 15,000 registered authors) was formed to address electronics rights issues. The registry hopes to make payment of royalty fees painless and help resolve any controversy.

If a solution to this ongoing disagreement is not found, authors may pull their works from online services. This controversy must be resolved in order to ensure maximum access to information.

International Issues

International legal concerns focus mainly on two issues—primarily about the Internet. The first issue is the export restrictions on cryptography. Second is the discussion about whether placing information on the Internet is "exporting" that data. The issues are very complex and confusing. Even different parts of the government disagree. For example, the U.S. Justice Department's Office of Legal Counsel has contended that export regulations regarding technical data and cryptography are not constitutional.

The U.S. State Department controls most cryptography exports; the International Traffic in Arms Regulations (ITAR) document contains the full set of export regulations. Cryptography is heavily controlled under these regulations, as if it were a weapon like a tank.

General noncryptographic information may also have restrictions. The U.S. Commerce Department controls general (nondefense) exports. General Technical Data Exportable to All Destinations (GTDA) are regulations for information exports. GTDA authorizes the export of information arising during or resulting from fundamental research and also authorizes the export of information that is publicly available, as well as educational information.

One additional concern is the interaction between local laws and international free distribution of information. The Internet's broad coverage raises unresolved legal questions. Can a discussion or posting that is legal in one locality be read in another locality where it is against the law? Can an information provider in California post information that a Tennessee district attorney considers to be obscene?

Database Rules and Restrictions

The professional researcher must be aware that legal rules and restrictions are placed in online sources. These include the personal use only restriction for Knowledge Index on CompuServe and the comprehensive (and) lengthy restrictions provided by Dun & Bradstreet for the allowed use of results from their databases. Some databases, such as Energy Science and Technology on DIALOG, have geographical restrictions.

It is part of the professional responsibility of the researcher to know and follow these restrictions. In addition, if the information is to be used by someone else, the restrictions must be passed on to the end user.

Vendor Liability

Another important issue is the potential liability of database vendors for quality. Currently there is a great deal of disagreement among courts on this topic. Ongoing lawsuits with widely varying results point out the need for reform and legal definition to obtain consistency. A potential added concern is the liability of a researcher.

Summary

There are many unresolved legal, ethical, and intellectual property issues associated with the Internet and online services. These unresolved areas include copyright in the digital world, electronic distribution, and international information transfer. Research professionals must monitor and influence the resolution of these issues.

For Further Reading

1. *Patents, Copyrights, and Trademarks*, by Frank H. Foster and Robert L. Shook (John Wiley, 1993). A readable and informative basic text on

intellectual property. A valuable resource that I reference frequently.

2. "Public and Private Domains of Information: Defining the Legal Boundaries," by Anne Wells Branscomb, *Bulletin of the American Society for Information Science,* December/January 1995. An interesting discussion of the economic value of information.

3. *Legally Speaking: The NII Intellectual Property Report,* by Pamela Samuelson, *Communications of the ACM,* December 1994.

4. "Is BNA Liable for Error in Proofreading? Company Says It Relied on Flawed Chart to Settle Case," by Gail Diane Cox, *National Law Journal* 17, no. 27 (March 6, 1995): p. B1.

5. "Liability for 'Soft Information': New Developments and Emerging Trends," by Richard A. Rosen, *Securities Regulation Law Journal* 23, no. 1 (Spring 1995): pp. 3–56.

6. "Unifying Tort and Contract Law in the Age of Data: What Principles of Liability Are Applicable When Defective Information Causes Physical Harm or Economic Loss?" by Michael Traynor, *National Law Journal* 17, no. 24 (February 13, 1995): p. B5.

7. "Online Services Fight Liability for Users' Violations: Look Who's Talking," by Susan Orenstein, *Legal Times* 17, no. 17 (September 12, 1994): p. 4.

8. "Whose Fault Is That Image? Liability of Database Providers," by Jon L. Roberts, *Advanced Imaging* 9, no. 2, (February 1994): p. 78.

9. *Netlaw: Your Rights in the Online World,* by Lance Rose (McGraw-Hill, 1995). A new book that appears to be a useful resource covering topics from First Amendment guarantees to rights of privacy.

An Introduction to the Copyright Law[*]

Copyright is a form of protection provided by the laws of the United States (title 17, US Code) to the authors of "original works of authorship" including literary, dramatic, musical, artistic, and certain other intellectual works. Section 106 of the Copyright Act generally gives the owner of copyright the

---

[*]Excerpted from Copyright Circular 01.

exclusive right to do and to authorize others to do the following:

- To reproduce the copyrighted work
- To prepare derivative works
- To distribute copies of the copyrighted work
- To perform the copyrighted work publicly
- To display the copyrighted work publicly

It is illegal for anyone to violate any of the rights provided by the Act to the owner of copyright. One major limitation is the doctrine of "fair use," which is given a statutory basis in section 107 of the Act.

Copyright protection subsists from the time the work is created in fixed form. The copyright in the work of authorship immediately becomes the property of the author who created it. Only the author or those deriving their rights through the author can rightfully claim copyright. Copyright protects "original works of authorship" that are fixed in a tangible form of expression. Copyrightable works include the following categories:

- literary works
- musical works, including any accompanying words
- dramatic works, including any accompanying music
- pantomimes and choreographic works
- pictorial, graphic, and sculptural works
- motion pictures and other audiovisual works
- sound recordings
- architectural works

Several categories of material are generally not eligible for statutory copyright protection. These include works that have not been fixed in a tangible form of expression. For example: choreographic works that have not been notated or recorded, or improvisational speeches or performances that have not been written or recorded. Other noncopyrightable categories include

- titles, names, short phrases, and slogans
- familiar symbols or designs
- mere variations of typographic ornamentation, lettering, or coloring
- mere listings of ingredients or contents
- ideas, procedures, methods, systems, processes, concepts, principles, discoveries, or devices, as distinguished from a description, explanation, or illustration
- works consisting entirely of information that is common property and containing no original authorship (for example: standard calendars, height and weight charts)
- works by the U.S. Government

Copyright is secured automatically upon creation. The way in which copyright protection is secured under the present law (since 1978) is frequently misunderstood. No publication or registration or other action in the Copyright Office is required to secure copyright. (There are, however, certain definite advantages to registration.) For works first published on and after March 1, 1989, use of the copyright notice is optional, though highly recommended. Before March 1, 1989, the use of the notice was mandatory on all published works, and any work first published before that date must bear a notice or risk loss of copyright protection.

A work that is created (fixed in tangible form for the first time) on or after January 1, 1978, is automatically protected from the moment of its creation, and is ordinarily given a term enduring for the author's life, plus an additional 50 years after the author's death. Any or all of the exclusive rights, or any subdivision of those rights, of the copyright owner may be transferred, but the transfer of exclusive rights is not valid unless that transfer is in writing and signed by the owner of the rights conveyed (or such owner's duly authorized agent). Transfer of a right on a nonexclusive basis does not require a written agreement. Transfers of copyright are normally made by contract.

There is no such thing as an "international copyright" that will automatically protect an author's writings throughout the entire world. Protection against unauthorized use in a particular country depends, basically, on the national laws of that country. However, most countries do offer protection to foreign works under certain conditions, and these conditions have been greatly simplified by international copyright treaties and conventions.

19 | *Secondary Marketing Research Using Online Sources Will Only Get Better*

> "Prediction is very difficult, especially about the future."
> —Niels Bohr

This chapter attempts to predict the future—a task mostly doomed to failure. However, there are important trends in the online information world that will continue to affect the performance of secondary marketing research. Secondary marketing researchers and information professionals should monitor these trends.

Knowledge Is Power

> More and more information will be required.

In the future business world, access and use of knowledge will differentiate the successful companies from the failures. Online information will be an increasing asset to the successful business. More end users will obtain superficial access to data. This will create an increasing demand for in-depth information.

Successful companies will be increasingly market- and customer-driven. Early involvement of marketing in product development will be pushed very hard. This will also increase the demand for information.

Changes Are Everywhere

> "Builders of the World Wide Web should be aware they are building a society."
> —Tim Berners-Lee, the inventor of the Web, speaking at the 1995 National Online Conference

Major changes will continue to appear in the online information marketplace. New companies and technologies appear daily. More people will become aware of the great variety of information accessible online. Dramatic changes have already occurred and will continue. You can now browse through the holdings of your local library—or of libraries halfway around the world—sitting at your desk at home.

The cost and pricing structure of information access will change as competition increases. Information access will be cheaper, and more transaction-based pricing will be available. Currently common charges for search time will be reduced or eliminated. However, information expenditures may remain relatively stable. As unit costs decrease, the amount of useful information increases—the same amount of money is then spent to obtain increasing amounts of information.

People will become increasingly comfortable using the Internet, and more information will be accessible on the Internet. For every database now available through the Internet, there are many that are not. Government agencies are only now beginning to connect their storehouses of information to the Net. Commercial vendors, from database services to booksellers, will increasingly establish an Internet presence. In my opinion, nearly all new Internet sources will be on the World Wide Web. The World Wide Web will get more complex, with more features as the authoring language (HTML) gets more features.

Trends in the professional services industry will be a continuation of existing trends, such as more full-text and image databases, improved currency (particularly as more sources are available on computer media), and more files that combine information from many sources. New search tools and pricing schemes will appear frequently—prices should decrease with more users and more competition. The overall information industry will continue to grow. Mergers and acquisitions will continue to consolidate the industry.

Telecommunications technology will improve, increasing the flow rate of information. ISDN technology will finally achieve critical mass—most Internet providers, Prodigy, and CompuServe will offer ISDN access. ISDN is considered to be the next generation of telephone service for voice, video, and data communication.

The consumer services will grow dramatically with the Microsoft Network entering the market. Surveys indicate that the online services market will rapidly gain membership in 1995 and 1996.

Consumers will become comfortable with using credit cards on the Internet—driving online shopping and new for-fee services.

The Great Dream: True Natural-Language Searching

Natural-language searching is the great dream of computer and database interface designers—particularly if combined with speech recognition studies. The hope is to achieve the conversational computer interface shown by HAL in the movie *2001*. While no such interfaces exist yet, impressive progress has been made. West, along with Dragon Systems, allows spoken access to their databases. Relevance search engines provide a first cut at near natural-language searches. Query by example will be a more common tool: if you get something you like, you can ask for more like it. Natural-language interface developers include ConQuest Systems, Delphi Consulting Group, and TextWise, Inc.

I expect that steady progress will be made here, particularly as processing power continues to increase.

Agents and Knowbots

> Knowbots are intelligent software agents that can be sent out onto the Internet or other databases and bring back requested information.

Intelligent agents or knowbots are the next step past natural-language searching. Now your home computer will not even need to be told what databases to search or be reminded of repetitive tasks. Every morning, your computer will make your coffee and assemble your custom morning paper. Since the agent knows your style and regular needs, it can provide the viewgraphs for your regular Friday meeting and plan your sudden trip just the way you would.

This will not happen next year—but people are working on it.

Summary

Online sources are now a valuable tool for secondary marketing research—quickly providing inexpensive and comprehensive data. As more information becomes available, search tools improve, and prices decrease, online secondary marketing research will become more cost-effective.

Expectations for information will rise with increasing end user access that will create demand. Information in the future must be timely, current, accurate, relevant, and affordable—all as defined by the end user's expectations.

Information professionals will still add value to information retrieval by providing such things as end-user training and information quality assessment. As end users realize that their time is best spent on their real job, more and more will turn back to the information professional for the most cost-effective access to information. (See references 3 and 4 in Chapter 3 for data on contacting information professionals.)

For Further Reading

All of us will be continuously barraged with stories about the changing online world. Newspapers, magazines, books, and TV shows will overload us with information. A useful counterpoint to all this is a recent book: *Silicon Snake Oil*, by Clifford Stoll (Doubleday, 1995). Mr. Stoll informs us of hype and hidden costs.

A good article about the growth of information markets is "New Markets for Information," by Thomas E. Miller, *American Demographics*, (April 1995). This article discusses the broadening market for information products—particularly in the home.

Index